microwave magic
the art of 21st century cooking

Written by
Jennipher Marshall-Jenkinson

Foreword by
Marguerite Patten OBE

Published by
MPress books

microwave magic
the art of 21st century cooking

Written by Jennipher Marshall-Jenkinson
in conjunction with:
'The Microwave Technologies Association'
www.microwaveassociation.org.uk
Foreword by Marguerite Patten OBE
First published in September 2006 by:
MPress© books, www.mpressbooks.co.uk
Photography by: Steve McDonough, www.smcfolio.co.uk
Food for photography prepared by
Jennipher Marshall-Jenkinson
Graphic Design by books@corecreative.info
Origination by: Andrew Marshall
Printed and bound in England by J.H. Haynes & Co. Ltd, Sparkford
Ovens for recipe testing and photography
provided by: NEFF, www.neff.com
Ovens used for recipe testing and photography were:
combination oven B6774 and mircowave oven H5642.
Cookware and accessories provided by:
Lakeland Limited, www.lakelandlimited.co.uk and
Wellbake Limited, www.wellbake.co.uk
ISBN no: 0-9551886-2-8   978-0-9551886-2-6

For: Mathew and Stephen

acknowledgements:
Andrew for encouragement, guidance and brilliant foresight.
Debbie's Digressers for keeping me sane over the past two years.
Nigel for an inspiration, Mary for continuous support.

The author does not accept any liability for injury or damage to microwave ovens or equipment in the preparation of any of the recipes in this book.

contents

thinking about...
the recipes in this book

All the timings for recipes in this book are based on 900 watt ovens. Like conventional cooking, however, microwave cooking times are approximate, due to the many differing cooking conditions that can be encountered. Stir food frequently as it cooks, as you would if it were being cooked on top of the stove. Always check food is completely cooked throughout before eating. Preparation times are approximate, where ingredients are to hand and do not include cooking times. All cooking dishes are microwave oven-proof.

adjustments to cooking times

Power settings used in these recipes:	Wattage	%	Change per minute
HIGH	1000	100	- 5 seconds
HIGH	900	100	No change
HIGH	800	100	+5 seconds
MEDIUM HIGH	750	75	+5 seconds
HIGH	700	75	+10 seconds
MEDIUM HIGH	600	75	No Change
MEDIUM HIGH	500	75	+5 seconds
MEDIUM	450	50	-15 seconds
MEDIUM	360	50	No change
MEDIUM LOW	300	30	-15 seconds
MEDIUM LOW	180	30	
LOW (gentle defrost)	100	10	

conversions:

25g = 1 oz
50g = 2 oz
125g = 4 oz
175g = 6 oz
225g = 8 oz
450g = 1lb
675g = 1 $^1/_2$ lbs
150ml = 5 fl oz = $^1/_4$ pint
250ml = 10 fl oz = $^1/_2$ pint
450ml = 20 fl oz = 1 pint

abbreviations:

tblspn = tablespoon
dstspn = dessertspoon
teaspn = teaspoon
All spoon measures are level

foreword by Marguerite Patten OBE

I am delighted to introduce Microwave Magic, for this is a book that is full of helpful and practical advice together with inspirational recipes. Jennipher Marshall-Jenkinson is an experienced Home Economist who, for many years, has helped countless people to enjoy using their microwave oven. As a full time working mother, she appreciates the importance of home-cooked appetising and nutritious meals and the need to prepare these in record time.

Please read the introductory pages first. These will give you the confidence to make the best use of your microwave oven. There is detailed advice on how to achieve perfect results when cooking each type of food. The right technique ensures succulent meat, poultry and fish together with perfectly cooked vegetables that retain taste, texture and nutritive value.

If at the moment, you use your microwave oven simply for defrosting frozen food or heating ready-made meals, you will be surprised at the diversity of dishes that can be prepared quickly and easily with available fresh ingredients.

Let me whet your appetite with a brief resumé of the recipes. Most of these will help you make first class family meals with the minimum of effort. In addition there are recipes for special dishes which will make sure you impress your guests when you entertain. Children are not forgotten, they will enjoy making the dishes on pages 77 to 82 An important section is for mothers of toddlers, the advice makes sure the small child has the benefit of freshly cooked food and mothers will be delighted by the ease which these meals are prepared.

At the start of the recipes, you will find satisfying soups and delicious pâtes. This chapter is followed by fish dishes. Most people would agree that fish cooked correctly in a microwave oven has a superb flavour. Two of my favourite recipes are fish in Paper Parcels (vegetables are cooked with the fish) and the more sophisticated Fish Roulade, pages 40 and 38.

I am sure you will approve of the interesting flavours given to various meats and poultry, which turn familiar foods into dishes of distinction. The sauces that accompany both savoury and sweet dishes are fantastically easy to cook in the microwave oven.

Have you ever thought you would like to make a special hot pudding or cake for tea, then looked at the clock and realised this is impossible in the time if you use conventional cooking methods? Look at pages 67 to 72 and see how quickly these are made by the magic of microwaves.

The results are excellent.

I have enjoyed Microwave Magic and I am sure you will too.

Marguerite Patten

microwave magic
the art of 21st
century cooking

thinking outside the box...
thinking and understanding inside the bubble...

introduction

There is no doubt about it, cooking habits of the British public have changed more during the last 5 years than they did in the previous 50!

85% of homes now have a microwave oven in them and this is set to rise again to 90% within the next few years**.

Families and lifestyles too have also changed beyond recognition, even over the past few years. It would be great if families could sit down to eat together every evening, but now if that happens just once or twice a week it's an achievement.

Most mums work these days and the pressure is 'on' to get a nutritious dinner on the table - usually within 30 minutes of arriving home, kids in tow - before they get to the crisps and biscuits. Cooking a mid-week meal isn't therefore a leisurely affair, it's essential for refuelling the troops before the next adventure or activity.

It has also been proven time and time again that mums do most of the cooking, so most cook in excess of 340 dinners a year on a budget, and attempt to make each one a little different. A microwave oven can really help take some of this pressure not only off cooking but reheating and defrosting as well, but for the food to be acceptable to every one who eats it, the user must possess some understanding of how microwave ovens work.

Today's microwave ovens and combination microwave ovens use 21st century technology to transform cooking. They are sophisticated, easy to use and produce excellent cooking results in a fraction of the time it takes to cook food conventionally. The old myths have been removed, like the fact that 'you can't put metal in a microwave oven'. Well you can - that's why there are metal racks and turntables in ovens today.

Yet, after being available to buy for over 40 years, microwave ovens are still considered a new cooking method. They often get taken out of the box, built in, put on a shelf or counter top, get used once, with disappointing results, then sit - unused, apart from waiting to defrost the occasional piece of food or reheat a cup of coffee. In short the owner does not understand how to make the best use of the technology in front of them.

The average microwave oven sold today has a wattage of 900. (Twenty years ago it was 600 watts). A higher wattage output oven might mean food gets cooked quicker, but often the quality of the end product is compromised. The perception that the higher the wattage of the oven, the quicker food can be cooked and eaten is technically correct, but the degree of success of the finished cooked or reheated product usually depends on whether the cooking instructions have been adhered to or whether (as most consumers do) the food has been cooked or 'ZAPPED' on HIGH power until 'it looks done' - which is guaranteed to give disastrous results.

For me 600 watts, or a MEDIUM HIGH power setting is the best one to use for most cooking. It is not over-powerful, aids even cooking and really adds only a few moments to the cooking time. But the end results can have enormous differences. Understanding is still the key to success with microwave cooking, reheating and defrosting.

The old adage remains - microwave ovens are still the most economical, convenient, and safe method of cooking known in the western world, but the user must understand their cooking process in order to make use of them properly. This book hopes to explain all. You will find some chapters are longer than others. These pages dwell on the 'good things' a microwave oven can cook, such as vegetables and fruit, fish, cakes and puddings, jams and soups.

Meat and pastry dishes are often better cooked conventionally then re-heated in the microwave oven, but all have a place in a 21st century microwave cook-book.

references

** - microwave oven penetration:
GB TGI, BRMB April 2005
Microwave ovens -
market intelligence
The Business Book 2003,
Independent Electrical Retailer.

understanding about... microwaves

there are four important facts to remember about microwave ovens:

- They are easy to use
- They are completely safe
- Their versatility and potential are boundless
- Cooking is faster and more economical than by traditional methods of cooking.

In fact the microwave oven is considered by the 'converted' to be as essential in the kitchen as a fridge, freezer or even a conventional oven. It is a very different method of cooking, but once the simple techniques have been mastered experience follows and the most demanding meals can be cooked as if by magic, in a fraction of the time it takes conventionally.

Desserts, for example, can cook while the main course is being eaten. Vegetables cook in the time needed for the meat and poultry to stand and rest before carving. Best of all, washing up is diminished to a fraction as some foods and meals can be cooked and eaten in the same dish. Vegetables for one can be cooked on the dinner plate, which also warms the plate; and dishes like scrambled egg and porridge don't leave a congealed mess in the bottom of the pan. The advantages of microwave cooking are endless; read on to find out why.

what are microwaves?

There is no magic about microwaves, they are created when the oven is switched on and are high frequency, non ionizing electromagnetic waves, (similar to television and radio waves) that were discovered by accident during the Second World War; during experiments with radar. On the spectrum of electromagnetic waves, the wavelength is located between the bands assigned to radio transmission and infra radiation - the ones used for infra-red grills in the top of ovens. Their similarity to radio waves is the fact that they are both very short waves, only 12 centimetres long, (hence the name - MICRO-wave,) and can be confined within the metal walls of an oven. Once the oven is switched 'On', electrical energy passes through a 'magnetron'. The waves produced are channelled into the oven by a 'waveguide'. These can be reflected, transmitted and absorbed - the properties that make them so useful. The waves bounce around inside the oven cavity, alternating in positive and negative directions through almost every substance except metal at 2450 megahertz (or 2450 million times per second).

If it happens to be food that the waves come into contact with, the molecules within the food react to the electrical charge by moving fast - 4900 million times per second. The movement produces friction within the food, which generates heat, but no chemical changes take place. It's a bit like rubbing one's hands together to keep warm - the resultant friction generates heat. It should be remembered though, that microwaves can

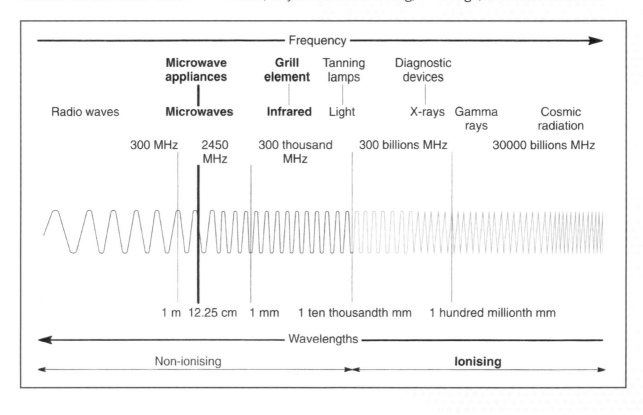

5

only penetrate up to 2.5 cms into the food itself. If food is thicker than 2.5 cms, the inner parts are still cooked by conduction as in a normal oven. So, microwaves cook from the outside in, not vice versa.

The magnetron will only produce microwaves when the timer is set, the oven door is closed and the power switched on. Every time the oven door is opened the microwaves automatically switch 'off'. Lastly, all ovens have a safety lock which prevents the door from opening accidentally.

thermal radiation from a grill element

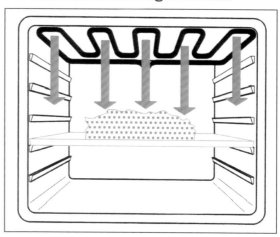

reflection on metal surfaces

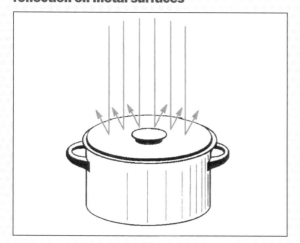

heat from microwaves

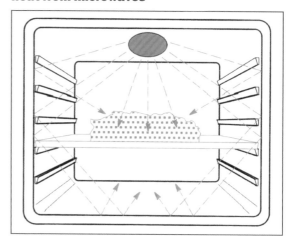

thinking about... successful microwave cooking

Many of the techniques used in microwave cooking are the same as used in conventional cooking, but these points help with a better understanding:

■ Ring shaped containers are ideal for microwave cooking, as energy can penetrate from the top, bottom, sides and centre. Round shapes can cook more evenly than squares or oblongs - which often absorb too much energy at the edges and corners.

■ Depth of food in the dish affects both speed and evenness of cooking. Food put in a shallow dish, in a thin layer, will cook quicker than the same amount of food in a deep dish of the same size and capacity. Choose dishes with straight sides, not sloping - otherwise the outside top edges will receive more energy and over-cook.

■ Arrange individual items like cups of custard, baked potatoes and bread rolls evenly on the turntable or oven rack. Leave plenty of space between foods, so that energy can penetrate from all directions.

■ Position foods with thin or delicate ends like asparagus, broccoli or chicken drum-sticks with the thick or tougher parts to the outside. These parts need more cooking, so will receive more energy and will enable the whole dish to cook evenly.

■ Cover any food that you would normally cover during conventional cooking, e.g. casseroles and vegetables. The lid holds in the heat and steam, speeds up the cooking and prevents the food from drying out. Cover bacon and fatty foods with paper towel to prevent the fat from splashing all over the oven walls.

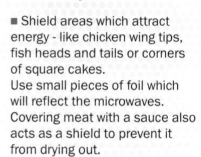

■ Shield areas which attract energy - like chicken wing tips, fish heads and tails or corners of square cakes. Use small pieces of foil which will reflect the microwaves. Covering meat with a sauce also acts as a shield to prevent it from drying out.

■ Elevate food while it is cooking on an oven rack or even an upturned saucer if no cooking rack is available. All food cooks better and more evenly if the microwaves have been allowed to penetrate from all sides, i.e. top, bottom and sides. By elevating the cooking dish/ container almost into the centre of the oven, the microwaves will be able to penetrate and circulate round the food quicker.

■ Make use of all your existing kitchen equipment. Paper towelling placed under bread rolls and pastries or even crumb coated chicken and fish absorbs excess moisture during cooking and helps to keep food crisp.

■ Stir food from the outside to the centre during cooking to equalise the heat and speed up cooking. Food will not scorch or stick, so it is not necessary to stir as often as in conventional cooking.

■ Re-arrange overlapping areas like tails of fish and closely packed pieces such as meatballs from the outside to the centre of the dish.

■ Turn foods over at least once during cooking. Large roasts such as chicken must be turned over, as areas near the top will over-cook quickly. Foods like hamburgers cook quicker and more evenly if turned during cooking.

■ Lower power levels as you would with conventional cooking. During microwave cooking, when the 'power' is off, heat continues to penetrate the food by conduction. A lower power setting also ensures that sensitive foods such as egg custards do not over-cook and the tougher cuts of meat in a casserole have time to tenderise.

■ Browning makes all food look more attractive. Food cooked in a microwave oven browns if it is cooked for longer than 20 minutes, due to the natural heat cooking currents. Foods such as hamburgers, chops or chicken pieces may be browned by coating with a blend of barbeque, Worcestershire or soy sauce, or even a sprinkle of paprika pepper. Cakes and biscuits can be finished with icing, or flavoured prior to cooking with carob, cocoa or coffee.

■ Casseroles can be given a crunchy top with toasted crumbs, crushed crisps, grated cheese or mashed potatoes then browned quickly under a hot grill.

■ Part cook chicken pieces, sausages or any meat in the microwave oven before completing its cooking on the barbeque. This way you can ensure the meat is thoroughly cooked and less likely to be raw on the inside and burnt on the outside.

■ Standing time is very important. Always allow at least a few minutes for this. It equalises the temperature throughout the food, and completes the cooking time. With meat, it allows the muscle fibres to settle, the juices time to run back into the meat and makes carving easier.

■ Wipe the walls and inside the door regularly to keep the oven clean.

■ Remove stale cooking smells by boiling some water in a shallow bowl, to which a little lemon juice has been added for 5 minutes. Wipe out the oven with a clean damp cloth. Any food stuck to the walls and ceiling can also be quickly removed; leaving a clean, fresh smelling oven.

is it done yet?

When you look into a conventional oven at a roast meat or chicken joint and you can see it turning brown and crisping up... you generally have a fair idea of when it will be cooked.

Ting! 'Is it cooked... Mmm, I don't know'... 'I'd better cook it for another couple of minutes. It couldn't possibly be cooked in such a short time.'

Ting! - 'Oooh, I think it needs another minute - it must be ready now. I'll serve it and see what the family thinks'.

'Mum, the meat is like leather, the peas like bullets and the carrots are like cardboard!' Sounds familiar? This Cook has a problem, and probably most of us have had the same thing happen. Overcooking is one of the biggest problems every new microwave cook experiences. The question is, how do you know when food is cooked to perfection, when colour is no indication of whether food is ready to eat? The most important fact to remember when cooking, reheating or defrosting any food in a microwave oven is that microwaves are attracted to fat, sugar and water - in that order - and that is what basically determines the speed and tenderness of any cooking product.

As is mentioned in many parts of this book, it is always better to UNDERCOOK food first until you are familiar with that particular recipe; cook it for a few minutes less than the recipe recommends and increase the cooking time gradually. Test the food before cooking it for longer and after standing time. Experience will tell you whether you have got the 'timing' correct for a perfect end result.

The reason for doing this is simple. Every type of microwave oven has a different wattage and a different distribution of microwaves, even with the same brand! As you often find with conventional ovens, each oven can cook slightly differently, so, it's a case of getting to know your own oven.

Also, every type of food has different moisture, fat and sugar contents and different starting temperatures; e.g. straight from the fridge, from the colder part at the back of the fridge, or room temperature. All this affects cooking times, much more with microwave cooking than by any other cooking method. They sound like small details, but it is important to take them into consideration if you are to get the best results in microwave cookery.

Even if your neighbour has the same microwave oven and cooks the same size leg of lamb, the time can vary. There might be more fat on one leg than the other, or the starting temperature might be different. Microwave cookery is quick, so it is important to check these things. If you do, you will get the best results every time.

meat
roasts

Meat can roast in a microwave oven, but it always comes out better if cooked using a lower power setting, as you would do if cooking it conventionally. It is easy to overcook roast joints, especially if you are not familiar with the quick times. It will take a little longer but if a MEDIUM power setting is used there is less risk of overcooking, the results will be very similar to that of conventionally roast meat, but still cooked much quicker and only slightly lighter in colour than conventionally cooked meat. You wouldn't set your oven on HIGH to roast conventionally, as the outside would become too dry before the centre has a

chance to cook properly. Microwave techniques are the same. Microwaves cook the food from the outside to the centre and only penetrate up to 2 - 3 cm into the food, so the centre of the meat joint is cooked by conduction. If you cook on MEDIUM power the outside will cook more slowly while at the same time allowing the heat to penetrate and the centre to cook gently. This 1.5kg gammon joint, was cooked, covered in 35 minutes. It needs to reach an internal temperature of 70°c, before cooking is completed. Cover then stand for 10 minutes before carving.

When cooking large roasts, it is a good idea to shield the ends with pieces of aluminium foil for the first half of the cooking time, this includes the thinner end of a leg of lamb. The foil reflects the microwaves and prevents cooking in these areas, while the uncovered areas continue to cook. Though don't cover the whole roast with foil as it will never cook! If the meat is tough after cooking then it has definitely been cooked for too long or with a higher power setting than is necessary.

Meat generally needs slower cooking to break down the connective tissue. (Connective tissue holds the muscle fibre together). Conversely if under cooked, the meat will not be tender and the juices will run red when pierced with a knife; not pink or clear as they should be if the meat is cooked properly; so could be dangerous to eat. Remember that a HIGH power setting will only toughen meat. Another point to consider is that microwave cooking is 'cool' cooking, i.e. there is no heat in the microwave oven to give the food added browning and crisping. It is only the fat in the meat that gives the natural browning. Looking at the meat and checking its colour and crispness is not a good guide to tell if the meat is cooked. The easiest and best way is to pierce the meat in the thickest part and watch the juices. They should be a pinky-clear colour, not red - but that also depends on how well you like your meat cooked - rare, medium or well done, though chicken and pork should always be cooked until the juices run clear and are well done. Internal temperatures of 77°c should be reached for lamb and beef. 80°c for chicken and pork.

If you take meat like lamb out of the microwave oven a little too early and start to carve after 5 - 10 minutes of standing time, then discover it is too pink for your liking, simply place 6 - 8 under cooked slices on a plate and cook on MEDIUM for 1 - 2 minutes to complete their cooking to your satisfaction.

Standing time is essential for all food cooked in a microwave oven, especially meat, as it allows the food to complete its own cooking, allows meat fibres to rest and tenderise, and equalizes the temperature throughout the food.

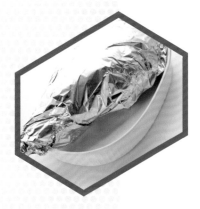

Meat roasted in any oven completes its cooking by conduction for up to 15 minutes after being removed from the oven. A temperature probe can be used to check the centre of

the meat is cooked thoroughly, but make sure the tip of the probe reaches the thickest part of the meat, and does not touch the bone.

It is always a good idea to wrap joints in foil while standing, so that the internal temperature is maintained.

Casseroles and smaller cuts of meat are best cooked on a lower power level, even MEDIUM LOW. Casseroles need a lower power setting, as they would if cooking conventionally. Ensure that the cooking dish is always kept covered so that the build up of steam inside the dish helps to soften the meat tissue and keep the meat moist. When reheating casseroles of more than one serving, reheat covered, on MEDIUM, and stir several times during heating. If heated on high the meat can start to cook and cause over-cooking. High power is really only suitable for reheating one covered serving. Great results are obtained when cooking meat joints in roast bags. Whole chicken and lamb for example, cook well in a sealed roast bag. Allow 8 - 10 minutes per 450g. The roast bag seals in the juices and heat so that the meat cooks thoroughly and evenly.

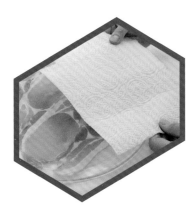

Thin meats like bacon, burgers, sausages and chops all cook well. See the recipe for Bacon and Egg bap on page 94 for instructions on how to cook bacon. Cook 2 or 3 chops and/or burgers on a MEDIUM HIGH setting for 2 minutes, turn over before completing the cooking for a further 2 - 3 minutes. Then leave to stand, covered, for 5 minutes to complete the cooking time. Don't overcook as the meat will toughen very quickly. The meat will be pale brown in comparison to conventionally cooked meat, but as you can see with the roast lamb on page 34, brushing the meat with dark marmalade, soy sauce, Worcestershire sauce or even barbeque sauce will add the desired browning effect whilst also keeping the meat moist and full of flavour.

These meats can also be part cooked in the mircowave oven, then completed on the barbeque. This is great for sauages that take an age to cook on a slow barbeque. It ensures too, that they are throughly cooked and so safe to eat.

poultry

There is less chance of poultry going tough and dry when cooked in a microwave oven because it contains less connective tissue than red meat. So, results with this cooking method are good if cooked properly, but again it is better to use a MEDIUM or MEDIUM HIGH power setting to ensure that the end result is moist and full of flavour. The meat is thoroughly cooked when the juices run clear when pierced

with a skewer, but again this must be done in the thickest part of the flesh - i.e. the back of the thigh. Always cook breast side down for the first half of cooking time and turn breast side up for the final part of the cook. This prevents the delicate breast from drying out.

Standing time is again very important. Always allow at least 5 - 10 minutes for this. 10 minutes plus if you have roasted the whole bird in the microwave - the larger the bird, the longer the standing time you should allow. A turkey will need 20 minutes standing time, wrapped in foil - perfect time to cook the vegetables in.

cheese

It is always best to use grated or finely chopped cheese in microwave recipes. This makes the cheese easier to distribute in the recipe and will provide a more even cook. Don't forget too that cheese contains approximately one third fat, so it can overcook and burn quickly, therefore always use a MEDIUM power setting, under cook it at first and test before giving it more cooking time.

eggs

Bad results come from overcooking eggs in a microwave oven - they turn to rubber! There is no one hard and fast rule for guaranteed cooking success, as every recipe is different, but generally eggs have to be treated with care during cooking. Use a MEDIUM power

setting and stir often. Room temperature eggs will cook more evenly than chilled ones.

The yolks of whole eggs will cook more quickly than the white, as they contain more fat. To prevent, say, a poached egg from exploding during cooking, prick the yolk with the tip of a knife and cook on MEDIUM power, half covered, so that the build up of steam can escape. Stop the cooking when the egg white is nearly set. Leave to stand for a few minutes, covered, so that the rest of the white has a chance to complete it's cooking. If still undercooked, you can always put it back and cook it for a few extra seconds. *Never try to cook an egg in it's shell, in a microwave oven.*
It will explode, sometimes even after being removed from the oven, due to the quick change of temperature both inside and outside the egg.

Scrambled eggs are not so critical in the cooking time, as the yolk and white are mixed together and this eliminates the problem of uneven cooking. They don't need to be cooked covered, but the cooking time should be stopped when the eggs are still runny in the middle of the dish. The standing time will complete the cooking. Remember though to whisk well 2 - 3 times during the cooking process for a light and fluffy result. Overcooked scrambled eggs are tough, and a watery liquid will start to separate them.

Omelettes are best covered during cooking. When cooking time is completed they will be set on the outside edge and have a small area in the centre that is still quite moist. Don't try to cook it until the centre is dry, otherwise on standing the omelette will be tough and inedible.

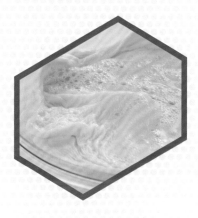

vegetables

As these are usually cooked in little or no water, or only the water that adheres to their surface, cooked vegetables are a lot crisper to taste than they would be if boiled in a saucepan of water on top of the stove. They do, of course, contain many more nutrients as well, as the vitamins and minerals have nowhere to go, so they stay in the food and are not leached out into the cooking water.

As they are cooked without added salt the flavour is intense and natural - which is often seen as a complaint - too much flavour, especially with Brussels sprouts. Though if you like really soft mushy vegetables, cook them conventionally, don't just try to cook them for longer, as all that will happen is that more of

the natural moisture will be evaporated from the vegetables as steam; the result will be dry and tough, often burnt and usually inedible. Most vegetables only need the standing time that it takes to get them from the cooking dish to the plate, but whole vegetables - such as jacket potatoes do require a standing time. However, they should be cooked until soft enough to be gently squeezed, or tender when pierced with a knife. Whole jacket potatoes should be cooked first and allowed to stand while other vegetables are cooked. By the time the other vegetables are cooked, the potatoes will be soft and ready to serve. If you wrap the cooked potatoes in foil for the standing time, they will also hold in their heat for at least half an hour.

If you like vegetables slightly softer, add 2 - 3 tablespoons of water to the cooking dish. As the contents of the dish heat up, the water evaporates as steam and assists with the cooking process, however you are not boiling water here, so don't add too much. Fresh peas and all types of cabbage benefit from a little added water as they contain less themselves. If over cooked, peas go hard and wrinkly. Make sure you stir well or give the covered cooking dish a good shake half way through the cooking time to help even out the cooking and give perfect results. Snow peas (mange tout), asparagus, carrots, spinach and the like have a naturally high moisture content, so should only be cooked in the water that

adheres to their surface. They should also be eaten slightly crisp to bring out their best flavour.

Frozen vegetables don't need additional water to cook them in, as there are enough ice crystals to keep them moist during cooking. Cooking times vary between fresh and frozen products. For example frozen sprouts take less cooking time than their fresh counterparts as they have usually been blanched prior to freezing, so only need partial cooking prior to serving. The same applies to swede, cauliflower and broccoli - if substituting frozen vegetables for fresh in a recipe decrease the cooking time by about 2 - 3 minutes.

Cooking dishes are important when cooking vegetables, more so than with lots of other foods. If you are cooking a large quantity, place the vegetables in a larger dish and stir or shake the dish half way through cooking time. If the dish is too small, the outside vegetables will start to over cook and the centre will remain raw. But don't put a handful of vegetables into a large dish; you will get uneven cooking due to the small amount of steam that will be given off in comparison to the amount of space that the steam takes up.

Whole green beans, asparagus and corn on the cob need to be spread evenly on the base of a shallow dish, so that the microwaves can penetrate evenly over their whole surface.

Don't forget that all vegetables need to be cooked well covered, so that the steam is kept inside the dish to help tenderise the food. If steam is allowed to escape during cooking the vegetables will dehydrate and end up like cardboard.

Lastly, if vegetables are over-cooked, most go hard from dehydration; some, like turnips go soft and limp. All over-cooked vegetables can be pureed in a blender or food processor or finely chopped and incorporated into soups or croquettes. They will still be nutritious and contain lots of fibre, and this way their appearance will be disguised.

cakes and pastries

Cakes are one of the most overcooked foods in microwave cooking. This is probably because the cooking time is so quick, it's hard to understand how they can cook so quickly!

When showing cooking techniques and to get the WOW! factor, I cook a circle of 6 fairy cakes on HIGH power for 1 minute, but at home use a MEDIUM HIGH power setting for both cakes and steamed sponge puddings. (There is nothing better than a microwave cooked steamed sponge pudding, it cooks in just 6 - 8 minutes. The secret to its lightness is to cover the pudding with greaseproof

paper throughout its cooking so that the steam cannot escape. This helps the sponge to rise more evenly).

A MEDIUM HIGH or even MEDIUM power setting means that you can control the cooking process better. Cakes cooked on HIGH power often cook too quickly at the edges and result in a raw, uncooked centre with hard, brick-like edges. For the best results: Always cook cakes on an elevated rack. This helps the microwaves to penetrate from the bottom and sides as well as the top and gives a much better and more even cook throughout the cake.

Bake until it looks set around the edges; if you touch the centre with a finger the top should feel slightly damp, but if you insert a skewer into the centre of the cake it should come out clean, so under the surface it is cooked.

The cake should also slightly come away from the sides of the cooking container. Place a piece of paper towel over the top of the cake and leave to stand for 5 minutes - the standing time will complete the cooking process. If the cake is still under-cooked after 5 minutes, leave the paper towel resting on top of the cake and cook for a further minute. Continue cooking in one minute bursts on MEDIUM power until cooked to your satisfaction.

Cakes won't collapse if removed from the microwave oven, allowed to stand then returned to be cooked for a little longer, but they will result in a completely cooked end product. To prevent fruit and nut type cakes from drying out once removed from the dish, allow to cool, then loosely cover with cling wrap. The remaining steam in the cake will go back into the cake and keep it moist.

Cook fairy cakes 6 or 8 at a time in small batches, in a circle around the outside of the cooking tray. Remember how little cake mixture there is to actually cook, and how much fat and sugar is in it, so cakes cook, dry out, then burn quickly. 6 - 8 cakes will never take more than 1 minute to cook.

When cooking oblong shaped cakes, use a MEDIUM power setting to even out the heating throughout the cake, and if necessary shield both ends with a little foil half way through the cooking time. This ensures that the ends do not overcook and dry out before the middle is cooked.

Pastry can be cooked in a microwave oven, but it remains grey looking. Pastry, when cooked, should be dry and opaque. If dark brown spots appear, the fat has started to burn and it is overcooked and will taste bitter. For a better end

result, it might be better to cook pastry in a conventional or combination oven and then use the microwave to reheat it.

Reheating cakes, pastries and breads

The majority of accidents and fires in microwave ovens are caused by over re-heating products like mince pies and sausage rolls to a point where they ignite or turn into bricks.

As I have mentioned before, microwaves are attracted to fat, sugar and moisture. Mince pies contain lots of sugar and maybe alcohol. If one mince pie is placed in the centre of the oven to reheat, it should be reheated on MEDIUM power for no longer than 15 - 30 seconds. During that time the microwaves will penetrate straight through the watery pastry part into the sugary part. Heating will be quick. However on touching, the pastry may still appear cold.

The pie should then be left to stand for another 30 seconds - this could be while it is being transferred to a serving plate. The heat from the centre sugary part will disperse into the pastry making it warm - but not soggy. The same process should be applied to sausage rolls and any

meat pies, to ensure that the centre is warm but the outside pastry remains crisp - not wet.

There is little fat in bread rolls, so when re-heating them, or any type of bread, take care not to turn them into rock hard bricks. Warm them on a MEDIUM or even MEDIUM HIGH power setting if you really need that extra 10 seconds in your life, but only for 15 seconds at a time. The steam you see escaping is the natural moisture in the bread. Once evaporated, all you are doing is staling the bread in record time by removing the moisture from inside it. We have all seen bowls of steaming bread rolls served to us in restaurants; they look and smell appetising at the time, but moments later become like golf balls when we try to break them open. All that has happened is that they have been over heated to a point where they have been ruined. 4 bread rolls should never take more than 45 - 60 seconds to reheat on a MEDIUM or MEDIUM HIGH power setting.

what about... defrosting?

Ask any one why they bought their microwave oven, and their answer will almost certainly be 'to defrost and reheat foods straight from the freezer'. It can take up to 24 hours to defrost food naturally, but a microwave oven can perform the job in under one hour, though like all other cooking procedures, understanding is the key to its success. Defrosting is best done slowly.

When frozen food is defrosted using microwave energy, the same friction that normally causes food to cook, encourages the molecules present in food to agitate. In frozen foods, the water molecules are present as ice; and as defrosting is carried out at a MEDIUM LOW or 30% power level, the microwaves cause the ice to melt rather than heat or cook; hence the reason for the 'standing or resting time' during the 'defrost' cycle. This allows the temperature throughout the food to equalise and defrost evenly.

here are some more tips to help with successful defrosting:

■ Always allow minimum defrost times - extra time can always be added if food is not sufficiently thawed. Excess heating though, using too high a power setting ruins food, as the outer edges may be over-cooked, while the centre is still frozen.

■ Elevate food to be defrosted on a rack. This allows the maximum amount of microwave penetration, from all sides and keeps it out of its own melted moisture, thereby allowing for a more even and quicker defrost.

■ Larger pieces of food may be defrosted on HIGH for 1 - 2 minutes, then the cycle completed on a MEDIUM LOW setting.

■ Take special care when defrosting poultry or pork, It must be thoroughly thawed before any cooking can take place.

■ Pierce skins and membranes before thawing to prevent them from bursting.

■ Turn food over at least once during the defrost cycle.

■ Separate blocks of frozen meat or fish, such as burgers, mince or prawns as they thaw to prevent them from cooking. As blocks thaw, they should be broken up with a fork so that the microwave energy can work more efficiently. Place the frozen pieces towards the outer edges and the partially thawed food towards the centre, so that they do not receive too much energy and start to cook.

■ Remove giblets from the cavity of poultry as it thaws. This speeds up the defrost cycle by allowing more air to circulate.

■ Open cartons and remove any lids and wrappings before defrosting, just in case they burst open during heating.

■ Be aware that home frozen food tends to take longer to thaw out than commercially frozen food. This is because the size of the ice crystals formed during home freezing are larger than in commercially frozen food.

microwave defrosting chart

Food	Time on MEDIUM LOW in minutes per 450g	Standing Times (Minutes)	Comments
MEAT			
Whole solid joints, e.g. beef, leg lamb, shoulder, loin pork	8 - 10	40 - 50	Shield anything thin or narrow ends with foil. Turn twice during cooking.
Minced beef	6 - 9	5 - 10	Break apart frequently. Remove thawed pieces as soon as possibe and leave to stand.
Steak, chops Sausages, burgers	7 - 10	5 - 10	Turn after half time. Shield ends and bones with foil.
Meat cubes, liver, escalopes	5 - 8	5 - 10	Separate and re-arrange twice during heating cycle.
Cooked, prepared casseroles	15	5 mins after half time, then 5 mins at end	Break up and stir thawed parts to centre as they defrost.
POULTRY			
Whole chicken, turkey, duck etc.	8 - 10	40 - 50	Breast side down first. Turn after half time. Shield wings, breast bone, drumsticks as necessary.
Drumsticks, wings, thighs	6 - 9	10	Turn and re-arrange twice during cooking.
Large portions - breast, leg and thigh	7 - 9	10	Turn and re-arrange twice during cooking.
FISH			
Whole trout, mackerel	5 - 8	5 - 10	Arrange in a single layer. Turn once during cooking.
Fillets, cutlets, fingers, steaks	4 - 6	5 - 10	Arrange in a single layer. Turn once during cooking.
Prawns, lobster tails, squid, crabmeat	3 - 4 per 225g	10 - 15	Stir halfway through cooking to re-arrange.
Boil in the bag fish	3 - 5	5	Pierce bag. Place on oven-proof plate. Turn after half time.
FRUIT			
Loose soft fruit - raspberries, strawberries, cherries	3 - 4 per 225g 6 - 8 per 450g	10 - 20	Measure out required amount. Heat stirring once. Stand until defrosted.
Loose hard fruit - apples, peaches, rhubarb	4 - 6 per 225g 7 - 8 per 450g	20 - 30	Measure out required amount. Heat stirring once. Stand until defrosted. Re-arrange pieces during cycle and standing time.
Purees - fruit deserts	7 - 10	10 - 15	Stir gently during cycle.
Cheesecakes with fruit topping, trifle, fruit pie	3 - 4	10 - 15	Stand on serving plate.
FLOUR PRODUCTS			
Bread - 1 large whole loaf 1 small loaf	4 - 6 2 - 4	10 10	Unwrap from plastic wrapping. Stand on paper towel, turn over at half time.
1 slice	10 - 15 secs	-	Place on paper towel. Time carefully to ensure it does not get too warm and become stale.
BREAD ROLLS AND CROISSANTS			
1 2 4	15 - 20 secs 30 secs 1 - 1 $\frac{1}{2}$	1- 2 1 - 2 1 - 2	Place on a paper towel. Time carefully to ensure it does not get too warm and become stale.
Pastry, uncooked, short crust and puff	1 minute per 225g pack	20	Remove wrapping, stand on kitchen paper. Check and turn frequently. Do not allow to get warm in places.
Filled flans 18 - 20cm (7 - 8 inches)	4 - 5	5 - 10	Set on kitchen paper on serving plate. Remove paper before serving.
Sausage rolls	2 - 3 minutes for 4	5	Wrap each in kitchen paper to absorb moisture. Standing time essential.
Whole light cream sponge cakes	1 - 1 $\frac{1}{2}$	20	Stand on serving plate.
Individual cakes: 2	40 - 60 secs	5 - 10	Set on kitchen paper. Standing time essential for jam doughnuts.

what about... reheating?

Most food reheats very successfully in a microwave oven, without loss of quality, colour, flavour or texture, but successful reheating requires a little basic understanding of the principles and techniques involved before food can be reheated to perfection. All too often, results are disappointing. The oven or food is blamed because, for example: the pastry is soggy, meat pasties and jam turnovers feel cold on the outside, but when a bite of the filling is taken, it burns your mouth, fish is dry and hard, meat, tough and leathery, vegetables dry and stringy, and breads and pastries stale. The list goes on..

As mentioned elsewhere in this book, microwaves are attracted to the fat, sugar and water molecules in food - in that order. They heat food from the 'outside in'. So, fatty or sugary foods will heat up quicker than watery or dry foods. I have explained in detail how cakes, pastries and bread based products react to over-heating in the chapter on 'Is It Done Yet?' So I won't cover it again here.

But, the answer to successful reheating is to think before you place any cooked food into the microwave oven. Use a power setting equal to one you would choose when cooking or reheating conventionally. If you stir a dish frequently in a saucepan on top of the stove (such as a can of soup or contents of a can of baked beans), then stir it periodically while in the microwave oven. In this way heat is distributed evenly and thoroughly and the food does not overcook or burn. As with all microwave cooking; always under-heat or under-cook food slightly. You can always put it back into the oven for an extra minute - but overheated or overcooked, food is ruined.

Bear these guidelines in mind when thinking about reheating food:

■ All food takes longer to reheat if it is chilled, If possible allow it to stand at room temperature for at least 10 minutes prior to heating.

■ Main course, meat and fish dishes benefit from a MEDIUM or MEDIUM HIGH power setting, so that the denser parts have chance to heat through evenly, remember to stir or re-arrange half way through the reheating time..

■ Always cover foods tightly during reheating, so that the moisture content is retained. Dishes that cannot be stirred (such as lasagne) should be reheated on a MEDIUM or even MEDIUM LOW power setting so that the protein parts (the cheese and meat) do not toughen and the pasta remains moist both during and after heating.

■ Individual portions of roast meat and vegetable dinners reheat most successfully. Carve meat into thin slices, place on an ovenproof dinner plate, cover with plenty of sauce or gravy to provide some moisture and prevent the meat from drying out. Accompany with vegetables of the same density so that they reheat in the same time (for example peas and carrots, green beans and broccoli, or potatoes and parsnips) and cover with a well fitting lid or cling wrap. Heat on MEDIUM HIGH for 3 - 4 minutes, until the underside of the plate feels slightly warm in the centre.

■ Lastly remember that all food needs to be served piping hot, so check it before serving.

microwave reheating chart

Food	Power Setting	Reheating Times (Minutes)	Comments
Individual plates of food:			
1 plate	MEDIUM HIGH	2 - 3	Meat portions should be well-covered with gravy. Plate covered with a lid
2 plates		3 - 4 $^1/_2$	Meat and bulky vegetables to the outside of
4 plates		6 - 8	the plate. Stand using a plate stacker
Cooked meats - Chicken pieces, chops, burgers, meat loaf:			
1 serving	MEDIUM HIGH	1 $^1/_2$ - 3	
2 servings	MEDIUM HIGH	2 $^1/_2$ - 4 $^1/_2$	Cover with cling flim. Re-arrange once.
Stirrable casseroles and main meals:			
1 serving	MEDIUM HIGH	2 - 4	Cover with cling film. Stir well after every
2 servings		4 - 6	1 minute
4 - 6 servings		6 - 10	
Non-stirable dishes e.g. lasagne:			
1 serving	MEDIUM LOW	5 - 8	Cover with cling film. Rotate dish at 2
2 servings		9 - 12	minute intervals
4 - 6 servings	MEDIUM	12 - 16	
Vegetables:			
1 serving	HIGH	1 - 1 $^1/_2$	Cover with cling film. Stir well at half time
2 servings		1 $^1/_2$ - 3	
4 servings		3 $^1/_2$ - 6	
Pies:			
1 whole family pie, chilled	MEDIUM HIGH	7 - 10	Set on an oven-proof plate
1 individual pie	MEDIUM HIGH	2	Stand on absorbant paper with another
2 individual pies	MEDIUM HIGH	3 $^1/_2$ - 4	piece on top
Pizza:			
1 whole individual pizza	MEDIUM HIGH	3 - 4	Stand for 1-2 minutes before serving
1 slice	HIGH	1 $^1/_2$ - 2	
Rice and pasta:			
1 serving - cooked rice	MEDIUM HIGH	2 - 3	Add a little stock, cream or butter to add
4 servings - cooked rice	MEDIUM HIGH	8 - 10	moisture and prevent food from sticking
1 serving - cooked pasta	MEDIUM HIGH	3 - 4	together
4 servings - cooked pasta	MEDIUM HIGH	10 - 12	
Individual curry and rice	MEDIUM HIGH	3 - 5	
Convenience foods, cans of baked beans, spagetti, etc			
200g	HIGH	2 - 4	Transfer to a suitable oven-proof dish. Cover
425g	HIGH	5 - 6	with cling film. Stir well after 1 and 2 minutes
Canned Soup			
200g	HIGH	2 - 3	Transfer to a suitable oven-proof dish. Cover
425g	HIGH	5 - 6	with cling film. Stir well after 1 and 2 minutes
Canned rice and pudding			
425g	HIGH	4 - 5	See above
Sponge pudding			
1 serving	HIGH	1 - 1 $^1/_2$	Cover with cling film, leave to stand for 2-3
4 Servings	MEDIUM HIGH	3 - 4	minutes before serving, especially if jam topped
Christmas pudding			
1 serving	MEDIUM HIGH	1 - 2	Re-Heat carefully, uncovered as high sugar and alchol
450g (1lb) whole	MEDIUM HIGH	4 - 5	content could cause pudding to burn if over-heated

have you thought about... accessories?

Take a look at this picture, then at the dishes already in your home, and the baking/grilling/cooking trays and racks supplied with your microwave oven. You have already got most of the cooking equipment needed for all your cooking needs.

But there is no doubt that some cooking containers are better then others. The right dish CAN mean the difference between a winner and a flop. Not quite as important when using

conventional heat from the convection oven, as any metal, china or glass heat-proof cookware can be used successfully, but it is extremely important when using a microwave oven.

Metal dishes and baking tins (including foil containers), can be used in microwave ovens, to cook food quite successfully, but they should be used with care. For example, try cooking two halves of a cake mixture, one in a

metal cake tin, the other in an oven-proof plastic container. The cake in the shallow metal container will take slightly longer to cook. However, you will find that it cooks more evenly, because the microwaves can only penetrate into the food from the top (as the microwaves bounce off the sides and base of the cake tin). So the cake cooks slightly slower and therefore more evenly. But take care, never stand the metal cake tin on a metal cooking rack. Stand any metal cooking container on a glass or plastic base to prevent 'arcing'.

So, you can put that lasagne in the mircowave to defrost and then reheat. Even if it is in a metal container. Just stand it on a dinner plate to avoid metal on metal (the foil dish sitting on the metal cooking rack).

Kitchen paper, basket-ware and wood should only be used in the microwave oven to hold cold foods that are to be warmed for a very short time.

Baby bottles - either glass or plastic - should never be sterilized in a microwave oven alone. When warming milk for baby in the microwave check the temperature of the milk before feeding.

Cling film, roast bags and the new 'steam cook bags' are invaluable aids to microwave

cooking, but make sure that the cling film you use is suitable for heating. Foods less than 2 - 3cm (1 inch) in depth cooked in shallow metal (foil) containers, e.g. lasagne, cook exceptionally well in a microwave oven and can be quickly browned under a hot grill for a better final appearance. As with the cake cooked in a metal tin, foil dishes ensure even heating throughout, so no hot and cold spots. They prevent the sides from boiling over and burning before the centre has achieved the required temperature, but stand the metal dish on a non-metallic plate during cooking to avoid 'arcing'.

Strips of foil can be used to wrap around the delicate ends of fish, drumsticks or the narrow ends of roasting joints (e.g. the end of a leg of lamb). Set in place at the beginning of the cooking time, then removed half way

through, the whole dish will be cooked to perfection at the end of the cooking time, without over-cooking or drying out the delicate ends.

If shopping for new cookware, look for versatility, design, size, weight, cleanability and value for money.

The best cooking containers to use are those which allow microwaves and heat to pass through quickly and efficiently. They should be non-porous and should not melt or warp when warm. Good dishes to use are: heat-proof glass, specific plastic cookware or ceramics.

what about... converting your own favourite recipes?

Everyone has standard favourites in their recipe collection - recipes that family and friends revel in almost every time they are cooked. Most recipes can still be cooked to perfection in a microwave oven and the following guidelines will help with converting them.

Always start with a recipe you are familiar with. If you have cooked it before you will know exactly what the finished product should look and taste like, so comparisons can be made throughout the cooking procedure.

Find a microwave recipe similar to one in this book to use as a guide. If the size of the main ingredients and the liquids are similar then use the same container, cooking time, power level and methods recommended in the microwave recipe. Leave out the oil or fat that you would use in a conventional recipe for browning meat or vegetables. You can add a small amount of butter or oil for flavour later.

Reduce flavourings and seasonings. Herbs and spices are stronger in microwave cookery because they do not cook for as long and there is less liquid present to dilute them, so taste and adjust seasonings, and add any salt just for flavour at the end of the cooking time.

If, on completion, flavours are still too strong, stir in a little natural yoghurt or soured cream into the dish just before serving. This helps to 'soften' the flavours.

Remember that microwave cooking time is up to two-thirds faster than conventional cooking times, but some foods take even less than this. Others, (for example like the cheaper cuts of meat in a casserole) can take the same amount of time to cook on a MEDIUM-LOW power setting, but there will be less washing up, less mess and less energy used during the cooking process. When the oven is on, using a MEDIUM-LOW power setting, only 30% power (electricity) is being used. For the remaining 70% of the time - even though the oven is in use, no energy or power is being consumed.

Foods that are naturally moist, or those which contain a robust sauce, convert well. Recipes where you would normally boil, steam, poach, cover or cook in liquid are very suitable for use in the microwave oven.

Reduce cooking liquids by one-third. When trying out the recipe for the first time keep some liquid to hand to add to the dish if required, but use just enough liquid to cover the dry ingredients, allowing for some to be absorbed. You can add more flour or cornflour to the sauces and gravies if there is still too much at the end of the cooking time.

When converting puddings and dessert recipes add one extra tablespoon of water or cooking oil to every egg used in a recipe. Microwaving extracts more moisture from baked cakes in the form of steam, so the finished result can be dryer if no additional moisture is added. Beat ingredients together only until well combined and lots of small air bubbles have formed. Over beating can cause the cake mix to collapse before the egg has had a chance to set the mixture. Sprinkle toppings such as bread-crumbs, parmesan cheese, crushed potato crisps, corn chips or grated cheddar cheese over food after the final stirring, to give casseroles a crisp interesting surface.

Always use large, deep, straight sided cooking containers for soups and casseroles, as they can boil up quite vigorously during cooking. To prevent boiling over, stir frequently during cooking. Remember a kettle of water will boil up quicker and more economically than water heated in the microwave oven, so if stock or water needs to be added to any recipe, use hot or boiling water from the kettle to speed up the process.

Cook casseroles which can be stirred, tender cuts of meat and chicken or minced beef on a MEDIUM to MEDIUM-HIGH power setting for speed without toughening the meat. If the meat is cooked in wine use less than normal, as it does not evaporate quickly enough during cooking, so the flavour of the sauce will remain sharp.
Use lower power levels for the tougher cuts, or delicate foods such as eggs, cream and layered casseroles. Pour off fat from chicken and other meats before finishing a sauce. Microwave cooking extracts more fat than conventional cooking (hence the reason why duck roasts so well in a microwave oven).

For soups and casseroles cut meat and vegetables into smaller uniform pieces. These ingredients will cook faster and more evenly.

It is better to underestimate cooking times and test often than to over-cook. Always allow for a standing time at the end as the food will continue to cook by heat conduction after removal from the oven.

Remember, selecting the best cooking method will ensure that all the food you cook will be cooked to perfection.

The following chart will help you choose:

Microwave only:
Soups
Fish
Rice, pasta, pulses
Scrambled and poached eggs
Quick sponge cakes
Some chicken recipes
Steamed sponge puddings
Sauces and custards
Vegetables and fruit
Jams and preserves
Bacon
Toasting nuts and coconut
Melting chocolate and butter
Softening cream cheese
Proving bread doughs

Combination only (microwave and convection):
Roast meats and Poultry
Casseroles
Gratin dishes
Pastries including choux
Pies, quiches, pizzas
Baked vegetables
Pre/part cooked foods that need heating and browning
Fruit cakes and heavier sponge cakes

Convection only:
Meringues
Long slow pot roasts

Grill only:
Steaks
Chops
Burgers
Toast
Crumpets
Crème Brule

Grill and microwave only:
Lasagne
Meat kebabs
Sausages

soups, pâtés and starters

Who makes soup these days when there are so many varieties available in the supermarkets that only need re-heating?

I do, because there is no comparison between the home made and pre-prepared versions. Home made soup is luscious, thicker and altogether tastier. If it's cooked in a microwave oven it will also be bursting with nutrients.

All soups and pâtés cook perfectly in a microwave oven, though they often take as long to cook as they do on the top of the stove, due to the pasta or rice in them that needs re-hydrating during the cooking process.

However the end results are always excellent, there is no direct cooking source, so the bottom of the dish won't burn - which is great for all those creamed soups. If the timer finishes and you have to leave the room, the soup won't boil over, - it will be at the same stage as when you left it, so just give it a stir and carry on.

For students, a large container of soup can be made for pence. Not to mention (again) the economical use of electricity. Youngsters cooking can be sure that it's a safe method of cooking, - a large bowl of boiling liquid being cooked behind a closed door, so it can't be knocked off the top of the stove by accident.

Last but not least of course is the eating! Flavours are enhanced so no salt needs to be added during the cooking process; more nutrients are retained as they haven't been boiled away, and less power has been used during cooking, as only a MEDIUM LOW power setting needs to be used once the contents of the pot has come up to boiling point. There are loads of cookbooks around containing soup recipes. All cook well in a microwave instead of on the top of the stove.

just remember these tips when cooking:

Use a large cooking container, preferably one that is deep and has straight sides. Stir well and often during cooking. This helps cook the soup thoroughly and prevents it from boiling over.

If converting a standard recipe, remember that very little evaporation takes place in a microwave oven during the cooking process, so cut down on any liquid added by one third.

Remember too that flavours of herbs and other spices are enhanced and remain quite strong during cooking, so use only half the recommended amounts. You can always add more if required.

Always add hot stock instead of cold to help shorten the cooking time.

Don't add salt until the end of the cooking time, then just add to taste.

Most cooked soups freeze, thaw and re-heat very well in the microwave oven. Cook an extra batch for future use. As re-heating is quicker in individual cups or bowls, line the bowls with freezer bags, add the soup, then when frozen, remove the bowls. When required they will be the exact size required for one or a crowd.

Creamed soups, or those containing egg, seafood, pulses or mushrooms, should be reheated on a MEDIUM power setting. Any higher could cause the soup to curdle.

french onion soup

If you are making soup in the microwave for the first time this is a great one to try. Inexpensive to make, yet it tastes delicious.

Melt the butter in a large 2 litre casserole dish on HIGH for 1 minute. Add the onions, stir well, cover dish and cook on HIGH for 4 - 5 minutes until onions are soft. Stir in the flour and continue cooking without the lid on the dish for 1 minute to cook the flour. Gradually stir in the stock, Worcestershire sauce, wine and black pepper. Cook, covered, on MEDIUM for a further 15 minutes, until the onion is really tender and all the flavours have merged.

Leave the soup to stand. Adjust seasonings to taste.

Place slices of bread under a hot grill and grill for 1 - 2 minutes until lightly brown.

Ladle soup into individual oven-proof bowls, add a slice of bread toasted side downwards and sprinkle with grated cheese.

Finish off by placing bowls under a hot grill until cheese melts. If no grill is available, just return filled bowls to the oven and cook on HIGH power for 1 minute until cheese has melted.

serves 4

preparation time 25 minutes

ingredients

- 50g butter
- 675g onions, peeled and finely sliced
- 50g plain flour
- 1 litre beef stock (may be made with stock cube and water)
- 1 - 2 tblspns Worcestershire sauce (to taste)
- 150ml white wine
- freshly ground black pepper
- 1 small French stick, cut into 2.5 cm thick slices
- 125g gruyère cheese, grated

tomato and courgette soup

This chunky soup is a meal in itself if served with crunchy fresh bread, Great if you have loads of tomatoes and courgettes left over in the garden; purée it then to make a smooth soup, which freezes well.

Place tomatoes, tomato puree, courgettes, half the boiling stock and the butter into a large 2 litre oven-proof dish or casserole. Cook on HIGH for 10 minutes, stirring occasionally until the soup comes to the boil. Continue cooking on MEDIUM for 10 minutes until vegetables cook and soften.

Meanwhile combine flour, black pepper, nutmeg and herbs in a small bowl. Mix to a paste with 150 ml water. Stir into remaining chicken stock, then into soup.

Continue cooking on HIGH for 3 - 4 minutes, until soup begins to boil and thickens slightly. If desired pour soup into blender and blend until smooth. Serve hot with a little fresh or soured cream.

Croûtons
Croûtons are another welcome accompaniment to soup - and easy to make in the microwave oven. Use wholemeal bread for the healthy option. They are also great to make use of left over bread that's beginning to go stale.

Melt 50g butter in a shallow ovenproof dish on HIGH for 1 - 2 minutes until bubbling. Cube 3 thick slices of bread and stir in. Cook on HIGH for a further 3 - 4 minutes, turning and tossing the bread occasionally during cooking, until the bread absorbs all the butter and crisps up.

Store in an airtight tin until ready for use, but do not freeze as this will make them soggy.

For a fat free option: place cubes of bread on a piece of kitchen paper, set on the oven turntable. Cook on HIGH for 3 - 4 minutes, stirring and re-arranging every minute until dry.

serves 4 - 6

preparation time 10 minutes

ingredients

- 675g tomatoes, peeled and chopped
- 2 tblspns tomato puree
- 4 medium courgettes, sliced
- 1 litre boiling chicken stock
- 50g butter
- 25g plain flour
- black pepper to taste
- 1 teaspn ground nutmeg
- 1 tblspn fresh chopped parsley
- 2 tblspns fresh chopped basil
- 150ml fresh or soured cream

savoury mushrooms with brandy

From the flavour of this dish no one would believe how simple it is to make, let alone that it is cooked in the microwave oven. But for even better results complete the flavours by browning under a hot grill until the cheese melts and begins to brown.

Place the bacon in a 1 litre oven-proof dish, cook on HIGH for 3 - 4 minutes, turning and stirring frequently until the bacon cooks and crisps up. Remove from dish, cover to keep warm and set aside to stand for 2 - 3 minutes, leaving bacon fat in cooking dish.

Add the butter to the dish. Cook on HIGH for 1 minute until the fat and butter bubble together, stir in the mushrooms and toss to coat evenly in the butter. Cover with a well-fitting lid or cling wrap and cook on HIGH for 2 - 3 minutes until the mushrooms cook but do not lose their shape. Stir in the bacon and pepper. Divide the mushroom mixture between 4 individual ovenproof bowls. If using fruit juice and not brandy, drizzle a little over each bowl.

If using brandy, warm in a small oven-proof bowl in the microwave for 15 seconds. Ignite, then when the flames die down pour over the mushrooms, cover each bowl with a topping of cream and a sprinkle of grated cheese.

Either put back into the microwave for 1 minute to melt the cheese, or set under a hot grill and cook for 3 - 4 minutes, until cheese melts and begins to brown. Serve immediately garnished with parsley.

serves 4

preparation time 7 - 8 minutes

ingredients

- 225g bacon, roughly chopped
- 50g butter
- 450g small button mushrooms, wiped and left whole
- freshly ground black pepper
- tblspns brandy or apple juice
- 4 tblspns double cream
- 50g cheddar cheese, grated
- sprigs of parsley to garnish

chicken liver pâté

A lot of people don't eat commercially prepared pâté for the fear of what's hidden inside it! That's another reason why I make my own. This recipe is easy to prepare, one of my absolute favourites and I can guarantee its flavour cannot be bettered.

Place bacon, onion, garlic and half the butter into a 1 litre oven-proof dish or casserole. Cook on HIGH for 2 - 3 minutes, stirring well half way through cooking time, until onion is tender. Stir in the chicken livers and black pepper. Cover with a well fitting lid or cling wrap and cook on MEDIUM for 7 - 8 minutes, stirring well occasionally until chicken liver has lost its pinkness.

Set aside to cool for a couple of minutes, set up the food processor, pour mixture into processor, stir in the brandy (or fruit juice) sour cream and extra seasoning to taste. Process until fairly smooth - but not too much.

Pour into a 500ml mould or 4 individual dishes and refrigerate until top is set.

Melt remaining butter in a small ovenproof dish on HIGH for 30 seconds.

Garnish pâté with the bay leaves and pour remaining melted butter over surface of pâtés.

If possible refrigerate overnight to bring out all the flavours.

Serve with melba toast.

makes approximately 500g

preparation time 15 minutes

ingredients

- 2 rashers bacon, rind removed and finely chopped
- 1 small onion, finely chopped
- 1 clove garlic, crushed
- 100g butter
- 375g pack chicken livers, trimmed and halved
- freshly ground black pepper and salt to taste
- 2 - 3 tblspns brandy or (if you must) apple juice
- 2 tblspns sour cream
- 2 - 3 bay leaves

potted cheese pâté

Lots of pâtés are difficult to make on top of the stove as they need to be cooked in a 'double saucepan' and need constant care to prevent them from burning. Cheese pate is another example of a great dish that cooks perfectly in a microwave oven. There is no direct heat source, so stir often to ensure the cheese melts evenly, cook on a MEDIUM power and make up your own variations: Stilton pâté is perfect with canapés; wholesome Cheddar cheese is great with a Ploughmans; Double Gloucester, Leicester and Wensleydale pâtés are great with crackers any time. This pâté is also great to use up lots of left-overs from the cheese board.

Melt the cheese, beer, half the butter and seasonings very gently together in a 1 litre oven-proof dish on MEDIUM for 5 - 6 minutes, stirring well every 1 minute, until melted and thoroughly combined. Remove from the oven and beat well until smooth.

Spoon into individual serving dishes. Allow to set in the refrigerator. Place a bay leaf on top of each dish. Melt remaining butter in a small oven-proof dish on HIGH for 30 seconds. Use to seal the cheese.

Chill well before serving.

makes enough for 4

preparation time 5 - 10 minutes

ingredients

- 250g strongly flavoured cheddar cheese, grated
- 3 tblspns strong beer
- 100g butter
- pinch mixed dried herbs, caraway seeds
- 1 teaspn white pepper
- 4 bay leaves

meat

Why do we cook meat? No matter what cooking method is chosen, the answer is always the same - to make it tender, more agreeable in texture and colour for eating, and last but not least, to kill of any bacteria that may be present, thereby making it safer to eat.

Microwaves, like any other cooking method, cooks meat, and like other cooking methods some make meat more palatable than others. You wouldn't grill a piece of shin beef, or breast of lamb. Microwaves also cook some cuts of meat better than others.

before going into specifics, here are some general guidelines:

Always ensure meat is thoroughly thawed before cooking so that the temperature throughout is as even as possible.

Cook whole joints, such as leg or shoulder of lamb or ribs of beef, sealed in roast/cook bags. The word 'roast' actually means to cook by dry heat. As you have read earlier, microwaves don't cook by this method, so

tenderising and making the meat safe to eat must be introduced another way.

Conventionally, roasts are generally cooked in a hot oven for the first few minutes, then the heat is reduced so tenderising can take place slowly.

The same applies to microwaves. Use a high power setting for the first 5 minutes, then reduce the power to medium or even medium low to complete the cooking time, so that a really tasty, tender joint is the end result.

Braises and casseroles also benefit from this cooking procedure, so that the long, slow cooking process has a chance to break down connective tissue and tenderise the tougher cuts of meat.

When testing meat with a thermometer ensure it penetrates the thickest part of the flesh to get an accurate reading.

When microwaving try to keep joints as evenly shaped as possible for an even cook. Shield narrow ends like the thin end of a leg of lamb with foil so

that it does not over cook. Don't cook joints larger than 2 kg in a microwave oven. As you now know, microwaves can only penetrate 2 - 3 centimeters into a solid piece of food, the rest being cooked by conduction. Joints larger than 20cms in diameter will not cook in the centre properly, before the outer edges start to dehydrate.

Trim away large lumps of excess fat before cooking, as this only melts and splatters all over the oven during cooking.

Re-arrange or stir meats like mince, chops and cubes of meat during cooking so they cook more evenly.

All meat benefits from standing time. It completes the cooking, evens out the temperature throughout, allows juices to settle, completes tenderisation and makes carving easier. Cover the meat lightly with foil to allow any steam to escape and prevent that 'boiled' flavour often associated with microwave roasts.

chilli con carne

Serve this with hot rice and salad. It's also a good filling for jacket potatoes and tortillas. Double the recipe for parties, or batch cook as it freezes well for a quick meal later. You'll also find that it's flavour develops on standing, so make it the day before, and leave in the refrigerator overnight. The next day you'll find the flavour more rounded but just as intense.

Put the oil and onion into a large oven-proof dish. Cover with a well fitting lid or cling wrap and cook on HIGH for 2 - 3 minutes until onion is soft. Stir in the beef, re-cover dish and continue to cook on MEDIUM HIGH for 5 minutes, stirring frequently to break up the beef.

Stir in the tomatoes, tomato puree, kidney beans and chilli powder (or sauce), stock cube and water. Re-cover dish and continue to cook on HIGH for 10 minutes, until liquid begins to boil. Stir, re-cover dish and continue cooking on MEDIUM HIGH for 10 minutes, stirring occasionally until meat is tender.

Season to taste and serve hot.

ingredients

- 1 tblspn cooking oil
- 1 large onion, peeled and finely chopped
- 450g minced beef,
- 400g can chopped tomatoes
- 4 tblspns tomato puree
- 420g can red kidney beans, thoroughly rinsed and drained
- 1 tblspn chilli powder or sauce - to taste
- 1 beef stock cube dissolved in
- 150ml boiling water
- seasonings to taste

shallot-tied oriental turkey

Use skinned and boned chicken breasts instead of turkey, but cut the cooking time down by a minute or so to avoid over-cooking and toughening the meat. I serve this with vegetable rice (plain cooked rice that has frozen mixed vegetables - sweet corn, peas, carrots and chopped green beans stirred through it) for a really easy economical yet very tasty dinner.

Flatten the turkey fillets between 2 sheets of kitchen paper with a meat mallet.

In a large mixing bowl combine all ingredients for marinade, add the turkey fillets and toss to ensure each fillet is coated with marinade. Cover bowl and leave to marinade for 30 minutes, or overnight in the refrigerator if possible, until most of the liquid has been absorbed.

Roll up the turkey fillets, securing each roll with tooth picks and tie each one round with the onion lengths.

Put rolls in a shallow oven-proof dish. Brush with honey and soy sauce glaze. Pour over any remaining marinade. Cover dish with a well fitting lid or cling wrap and cook on MEDIUM HIGH for 8 - 10 minutes, turning rolls over and re-glazing half way through cooking time. Leave to stand for 2 - 3 minutes.

Combine cornflour with 1 tablespoon of water, then stir into cooking liquor. Cook on HIGH for 1 minute until sauce thickens. Just before serving, glaze turkey with sauces.

Put rolls on a warm serving plate, cover and leave to stand for 2 - 3 minutes before serving.

serves 4

preparation time 10 minutes

ingredients

- 2 turkey fillets, cut in half to give 4 thin slices
- 8 shallots (spring onions) cut into 15cm lengths and halved lengthwise
- 1tblspn honey
- 1tblspn dark soy sauce

marinade:

- 1 tblspn lemon juice
- 1 teaspn bicarbonate of soda
- 2 tblspns dark soy sauce
- 1 tblspn honey
- few drops sesame oil
- 1 extra spring onion, chopped
- 1 teaspn ground ginger
- 1 teaspn cornflour

glazed ham

Gammon actually roasts very well in the microwave oven, but make sure you check it's weight before cooking to calculate the correct cooking time. A one kilo joint serves approximately 6 - 8 people, but as with all hams it's great served cold in sandwiches or salads later.

Weigh the meat to calculate cooking time. (Allow 8 - 10 minutes per 450g).

Score the surface of the meat with diagonal cuts (cut only 1 cm deep). Stud each square with a whole clove. Place meat in a shallow oven-proof dish.

Mix juice from the can of pineapple with remaining ingredients in an oven-proof jug. Heat on HIGH for 2 minutes until sugar dissolves and liquid boils. Spoon glaze carefully over ham.

Cover meat with cling wrap and cook on MEDIUM for 30 - 35 minutes, basting ham with glaze every 10 minutes, until internal temperature reaches 70°C and a knife inserted into the centre of the meat comes out clean and easily. Carefully replace cling wrap after each glazing to ensure that surface does not dry out.

Remove meat from dish, pour remaining glaze over meat, garnish with pineapple rings, cover with foil and allow to stand for 10 minutes before serving.

serves 6 - 8

preparation time 15 minutes

ingredients

- 1 - 1 ½ kg joint of gammon (unsmoked)
- a few whole cloves
- 411g can sliced pineapple in natural juice
- 50g dark soft brown sugar
- 1 teaspn prepared mustard
- 1 tblspn wine vinegar
- 1 tblspn honey

chicken and bacon terrine

The colours of this dish really show how microwaves can cook meat to perfection whilst also bringing out all the brightness of the herbs. Serve this hot with new potatoes and long green beans, or it is really lovely if served cold with a salad as a starter.

Put the butter and onion into an oven-proof bowl. Cover with a well fitting lid or cling wrap and cook on HIGH for 2 minutes, until onion softens. Stir in chopped apricots, breadcrumbs, parsley, pine nuts and horseradish cream. Add seasonings to taste and set aside.

Flatten the chicken breasts between 2 sheets of kitchen paper with a meat mallet. Stretch the bacon across the back of a knife and use to line a 500g loaf dish.

Place a layer of chicken over the bacon, then cover with half the apricot filling. Cover with another layer of chicken, then remaining apricot filling. Finish remaining chicken. Fold over with remaining bacon rashers to seal dish together.

Cover dish with cling wrap and cook on MEDIUM HIGH for 8 - 10 minutes, until chicken juices run clear and a knife slips through meat cleanly. Temperature at the centre of the meat should be 80°C.

Leave to stand for 2 - 3 minutes, then turn terrine out of dish on to a serving plate. Leave loaf dish covering terrine, while glaze is made.

Drain off any excess meat juices and in a small bowl combine with apricot jam and vinegar. Cook on HIGH for 30 seconds, stir well then use to coat terrine.

serves 4 as a starter or 3 as a main course

preparation time 30 minutes

ingredients

- 25g butter
- 4 spring onions, finely sliced
- 125g dried, ready to eat apricots, roughly chopped
- 25g white breadcrumbs
- 2 tblspns chopped basil or parsley
- 25g pinenuts
- 1 teaspn creamed horseradish
- 6 rashers streaky bacon
- 3 chicken breasts or 6 chicken thighs, skinned and boned
- seasonings to taste

glaze:

- 1 tblspn apricot jam
- 1 teaspn wine vinegar

tangy roast lamb

Spring Lamb roasts beautifully in the microwave oven. Leg is a tender cut. Cooked carefully it is juicy, moist and full of flavour. Shoulder joints taste just as good, though contain slightly more fat and take a few minutes more to cook and tenderise. The acidic marmalade added to this recipe not only helps tenderise it during cooking but also gives a tasty tang to the meat and sauce.

Brush the lamb with the warmed marmalade and place in an oven-roasting bag, set this in an oven-proof dish. Add the onion and sprigs of mint to the bag. Seal and cook on HIGH for 5 minutes.

Gently turn meat over and continue to cook on MEDIUM for 25 minutes. Test by inserting a skewer or sharp knife into the centre of the meat; the juices should run mostly clear. If using a meat thermometer the temperature should reach 65°C. This meat is now cooked medium. For well done meat, cook on MEDIUM for a further 10 minutes to raise the internal temperature to 70°C. Juices should now run clear when pierced with a knife.

Carefully remove meat from cooking bag, wrap loosely in foil and leave to stand for 10 minutes.

Meanwhile, drain the juices from the bag into a small oven-proof bowl, allow fat to rise to the surface and skim off. Stir the mint sauce, additional marmalade and cornflour, (blended with little cold water) into juices. Cook sauce on HIGH for 2 - 3 minutes, stirring after 1 minute until liquid boils and thickens.

Serve sauce as an accompaniment to the lamb, with a little poured over meat.

serves 4 - 6

preparation time 10 minutes

ingredients

- 1 - 1 ½ kg leg of spring lamb
- 2 tblspns marmalade, warmed
- 1 onion, sliced
- handful of fresh mint leaves
- 1 tblspn prepared mint sauce
- additional 1 tblspn marmalade (with lots of shreds)
- 1 teaspn cornflour

fish

I must admit, in my opinion, it's hard to beat the flavour of fish cooked in the microwave oven. Microwaves really do cook fish to perfection in the quickest of times. The results are always superb, fresh, moist and tasty, with the minimum of effort and washing up - not to mention no fishy smells around the house.

Fish and shell fish cook very quickly in the microwave oven because of their high moisture content. As the microwaves are attracted to the moisture, fish cooks quickly, so if in doubt always undercook and check frequently to see if the cooking process is complete.

For a quick nutritious meal for one, add a knob of butter and a dash of lemon juice to a fillet or fish steak. Place in a shallow ovenproof dish, cover and cook on MEDIUM HIGH power for 2 - 3 minutes. Leave to stand for a

further 1 - 2 minutes before serving. What could be easier!

Here are a few simple guidelines to achieve the best cooking results for both fresh and frozen fish:

Fish loses it's moisture quickly during cooking, so always cover the dish with a well fitting lid or cling wrap before cooking.

Arrange fish so that thicker pieces are towards the outside of the dish and the thinner pieces are towards the centre. This makes for more even cooking and prevents the thinner parts from drying out during cooking. If necessary fold the tail end of large fillets under the thick ends to give a uniform depth and ensure even cooking.

When cooking any whole fish - trout, mackerel etc. lightly score the skin of the flesh at the thickest parts to allow the steam

inside to escape.

Fish cooked with heads and tails left intact require the thin tails to be wrapped to prevent them from breaking off. Always cook fish in a non-metallic container, such as a shallow casserole dish, oven bag or specific microwave cookware. Shallow metallic containers are suitable for cooking fish in the microwave, but the fish can often absorb the flavours and sometimes take on a metallic taste.

Where liquids are not used during cooking always dot the fish with butter or brush it with olive oil to keep it moist.

Always under-cook rather than over-cook fish. Remember, due to heat retention it continues to cook a little after removal from the oven. Over-cooked fish is dry, tough and stringy.

Never season with salt until after the cooking time. Salt absorbs the natural moisture from the fish and will toughen it quickly.

If fish is frozen it can be thawed using the DEFROST or MEDIUM LOW setting prior to cooking. Ensure that the fillets and steaks are separated during the thawing process so that the thinner parts do not start to cook before the thicker parts thaw out, and leave to stand for as long as possible prior to cooking. When poaching fish avoid adding too much extra liquid as microwave energy tends to concentrate on the liquid rather than the fish. This can also toughen the fish due to prolonged cooking.

Timing is most important when cooking fish. It is cooked when white or opaque and flakes easily with a fork when pressed at the thickest parts.

Shell fish is cooked when transparent flesh becomes white, and the shells on crustaceans become orange-red in colour.

If fish is dry and very flaky it is over cooked, but don't waste it - mash it and use to make fish cakes.

To remove fish odours from the oven after cooking, heat a bowl of water containing cut lemon slices on HIGH power for 6 - 8 minutes, then wipe out oven using a clean damp cloth.

a few don'ts:

Don't attempt to deep fat fry fish or any other food in a microwave oven - it's impossible to regulate the rate of heating the fat, so it could boil up and over very quickly - very dangerous!
Don't try to cook live seafood - e.g. lobster in a microwave oven. Kill it first by plunging into gently simmering water. To cook, cut in half, place both halves in a shallow oven proof dish, cover and cook for 5 - 6 minutes on MEDIUM HIGH power for each 500g of flesh.

Shellfish such as prawns are great cooked in their shells, as microwaves are able to pass through the shells unhindered and help to keep the fish moist.

Don't attempt to cook fish in batter or breadcrumbs in a microwave oven. It just doesn't work!

defrosting and cooking times for fish

Power settings	Weight	Defrost time at medium low	Cooking time at medium high
Small whole fish	225g	10 minutes	4 - 5 minutes
Large whole	1 kg	25 minutes	10 - 12 minutes
Fish fillets	450g	13 minutes	6 - 7 minutes
Fish Cutlets	450g	15 minutes	7 - 8 minutes
Whole prawns	450g	15 minutes	6 - 8 minutes (peeled)

serves 4 - 6

preparation time 10 minutes

ingredients

- 25g butter
- 1 large onion, sliced
- 3 leeks thoroughly washed and thinly sliced
- 2 carrots, peeled and thinly sliced
- 1 stick celery, roughly chopped
- 1 green pepper, deseeded and thinly sliced
- 1 litre boiling fish stock (may be made with stock cube and water)
- 1 bay leaf
- 1 teaspn thyme
- 4 large sprigs fresh parsley, washed
- pinch powdered saffron
- 2 cloves garlic, crushed (optional)
- 450g fish fillet or fish steaks, cut into large chunks
- 100g cooked prawns, shelled
- black pepper to taste

seafood soup

A lovely versatile recipe this one. Choose fish of your choice - this could be a mixture of fresh white or smoked fish, or even salmon. It's also good to use up lots of end tail pieces that the fish counters often sell off by the half-kilo. The soup freezes well, so make up this quantity, eat some and freeze the remainder in serving portions for one to eat later.

Place butter, onion, leeks, carrot, celery and pepper in a large 2 - 3 litre ovenproof dish or casserole. Cover with a well fitting lid or cling wrap and cook on HIGH for 2 minutes, stir well to distribute the melting butter then continue to cook on HIGH for 3 minutes. Stir in boiling fish stock, herbs and garlic. Continue to cook covered on HIGH for 5 minutes, to complete the cooking of the vegetables and bring out the flavours of the herbs.

Stir well, then gently add fish. Re-cover and cook on HIGH for a further 5 - 7 minutes. Stir in the prawns. Cook on HIGH for 1 minute so that prawns are heated through, but do not have a chance to toughen or over-cook. Adjust seasonings to taste, remove parsley stalks.

Serve immediately with lots of fresh crusty bread.

fish roulade

**Absolutely my most favourite gourmet fish dish - it looks beautiful, yet is simplicity itself to prepare!
Serve it hot or cold with vegetables or salad.**

Whip the 4 tablespoons of cream in a medium sized bowl until stiff. Whip the egg whites in another bowl until stiff and dry. Whip the egg yolks in a small bowl until frothy. Fold the egg whites, yolks, well drained crabmeat and seasoning into the cream. Place in refrigerator until required.

Cook the washed spinach leaves in a small ovenproof dish or casserole covered with a well fitting lid or cling wrap with only the water that adheres to its leaves on HIGH for 2 - 3 minutes until just tender. Drain and set aside.

Place a piece of cling wrap on a flat work surface. Lay the white fish fillets on wrap so that they form a rectangle approximately 30 x 25cm. Place the spinach leaves evenly over the top of fish, then spoon over crab mixture. (Do not spread crab mixture too thickly, as it will ooze out of roll before cooking. Any remaining mixture can be cooked in a small greased oven-proof dish separately.)

Cover crab mixture with a layer of smoked salmon. Roll up the fish in Swiss roll fashion, using cling wrap as a guide. When rolled, carefully wrap cling wrap around fish to secure. Lift into a large shallow oblong ovenproof dish. Cook on MEDIUM HIGH for 5 minutes. Test with a sharp knife or skewer to see if fish is cooked. Cover dish with foil and leave to stand and rest for 15 minutes before slicing.

To make the sauce: melt the butter in a 1 litre oven proof jug on HIGH for 1 minute, add flour and stir well. Stirring continuously, gradually add the stock and wine. Cook on HIGH for 2 - 3 minutes stirring every minute, until the sauce boils and thickens. Stir in cream and peppercorns.

Unwrap fish roulade from cling wrap and slice into 1 - 2 cm slices, arrange on serving plate accompanied with the sauce.

Serve with a crisp green salad

serves 4 - 6

preparation time -
25 minutes, excluding standing time

ingredients

- 4 tblspns double cream
- 2 eggs, separated
- 170g can crabmeat, well drained
- black pepper to taste
- 225g fresh spinach leaves, stalks removed and thoroughly washed
- 5 thinly sliced white fish fillets (e.g. plaice)
- 200g smoked salmon, thinly sliced

sauce:

- 1 tblspn butter
- 1 tblspn plain flour
- 150 ml chicken stock
- 2 tblspns white wine
- 125 ml double cream
- 2 teaspns coloured peppercorns, lightly crushed

monk fish on rosemary skewers

Thick chunky monk fish is a real indulgence, and cooks perfectly in the microwave oven. It is delicious with this herby lemon glaze, but make sure you remove the tough pinkish-grey membrane covering the fish before cooking, otherwise it will shrink and toughen the fish. The rosemary skewers are a real novelty too. Use chunky fillets of cod instead of monk fish for a less expensive substitute; it will take the same time to cook. Reduce cooking time to 3 - 4 minutes if cooking a single portion for one or increase the cooking time to 8 - 10 minutes if doubling the recipe to serve 4 people.

Combine the olive oil, lemon juice, chopped rosemary and parsley together in a small bowl.

Strip the leaves off the rosemary stalks to make skewers, leaving a little sprig of leaves on the top of each stalk. Thread the fish on to each stalk. Place skewers on to a shallow oven proof dish or plate.

Brush fish with oil and lemon juice mixture. Cover with a well fitting lid or cling wrap and cook on MEDIUM for 5 - 6 minutes, re-glaze with oil and lemon juice, half way through cooking time. Cook until fish is just beginning to flake, when pressed, with a sharp knife. Leave covered to stand for 3 - 4 minutes to complete it's cooking time.

Serve on a bed of green salad and garnished with lemon wedges.

serves 2

preparation time 10 minutes

ingredients

- 2 tblspns olive oil
- juice $1/2$ lemon
- 1 tblspn rosemary, roughly chopped
- 1 tblspn parsley, roughly chopped
- 4 stalks rosemary, about 18cms long
- 350g monk fish, cut into large chunks

fish in paper parcels

Even the kids love this one, as they can unwrap the 'parcel' themselves - it's a great midweek meal. Use large chunky pieces of any white fish or salmon, that have been skinned and boned.
Double the recipe for 4 people and cook parcels for 6 minutes, or halve recipe for one and cook for 3 minutes.

Cut the carrot, onions and celery into thin matchsticks. Put the butter and vegetables into a medium sized ovenproof dish, cover and cook on HIGH for 2 minutes or until just soft. Season with pepper if desired.

Meanwhile cut 2 rectangles of greaseproof or baking paper, large enough to wrap one piece of fish in plus the vegetables.

Put a piece of fish on each piece of paper and top with the vegetables and their buttery juices. Sprinkle parsley over the top. Loosely fold the paper over the fish, tucking in the ends underneath to make neat parcels. Place on an oven-proof plate.

Cook on MEDIUM HIGH for 4 minutes until the fish is cooked.

Serve with rice and green vegetables

serves 2
preparation time 6 - 8 minutes

ingredients

- 1 medium carrot, peeled
- 3 spring onions, trimmed
- 2 celery stalks
- 25g butter
- fresh ground pepper
- 2 fish portions, - about 175g each
- 1 tblspn fresh chopped parsley

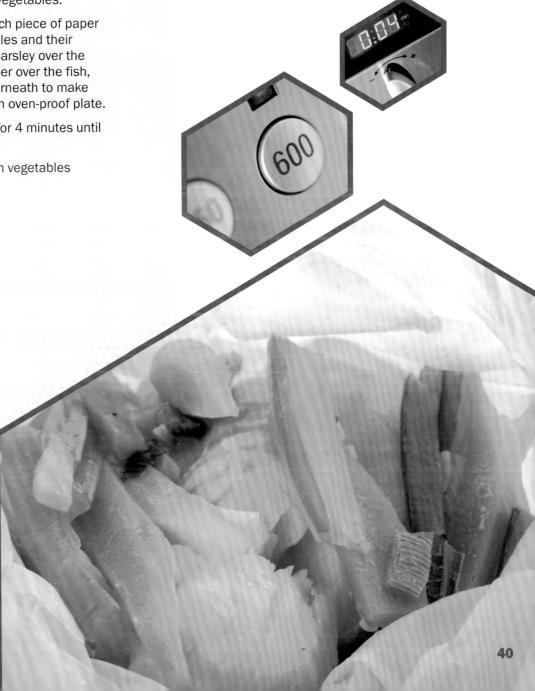

kedgeree

Another one of my great standbys ideal for lunch or dinner - and it freezes well for an even quicker meal later on!
Use 1 cup of rice to 2 cups of liquid - the rice cooks perfectly in that amount of liquid, as long as you use the same sized cup for both measurements.

Boil the eggs on top of the stove for 6 - 8 minutes until hard boiled. Rinse under cold running water for 2 - 3 minutes to cool, then set aside.

Meanwhile, put the fish into a shallow ovenproof dish, cover with a well fitting lid or cling wrap and cook on MEDIUM HIGH for 3 - 4 minutes until the fish is cooked, and when pressed with the end of a knife the flesh just flakes away. Leave to cool while the rice is being prepared.

Place the well washed rice, boiling water, stock cube, black pepper and turmeric into a large oven-proof dish or casserole. Cook on HIGH for 10 minutes, stirring half way through cooking time Reduce power to MEDIUM and continue cooking for 5 minutes until all the water has been absorbed and the rice is cooked. Stir the butter through the rice.

While rice is cooking, roughly chop the eggs, remove the skin from the fish and roughly flake.

Stir the eggs and fish gently through the rice. Set on a warm serving plate, garnish with the spring onions and lemon wedges.

serves 2 - 3

preparation time 25 minutes

ingredients

- 2 eggs
- 450g smoked haddock fillets, washed
- 125g (1 cup) long grain rice, well washed
- 500ml (2 cups) boiling water (or fish stock)
- 1 fish stock cube
- fresh ground black pepper
- 1 heaped teaspn turmeric
- 50g butter
- 2 - 3 spring onions, finely chopped
- 1 lemon, cut into wedges

pesto garlic prawns

A great dish to cook in the microwave oven. Flavours are fresh and bright, and if left to the last minute to cook can form part of a fabulous dinner party, not to mention a quick if extravagant lunch when served with lots of fresh crusty bread. Use raw prawns - the larger you can afford the better, but if you must use cooked ones, remember they only need a quick reheat for 2 - 3 minutes on MEDIUM. Re-cooking will mean that they toughen and lose that gorgeous flavour.

Place butter in a large shallow ovenproof dish or casserole. Melt on HIGH for 30 seconds, stir in the pesto sauce, lemon juice and garlic. Gently add prawns and toss to coat with butter.

Cover dish with a well fitting lid and cook on MEDIUM for 6 - 8 minutes, giving dish a good shake or stir half way through cooking time.

Prawns are cooked when they are pink and opaque, and solid throughout when pierced with a sharp knife.

Check if they are cooked after the minimum cooking time as they really do toughen if overcooked.

Serve immediately, garnished with fresh basil leaves.

serves 4
preparation time 5 minutes

ingredients

- 50g butter
- 2 tblspns prepared pesto sauce
- 2 tblspns lemon juice
- 2 cloves garlic, crushed
- 500g shelled, cleaned,
- raw king prawns (approximately 750g of prawns in the shell)
- basil leaves for garnish

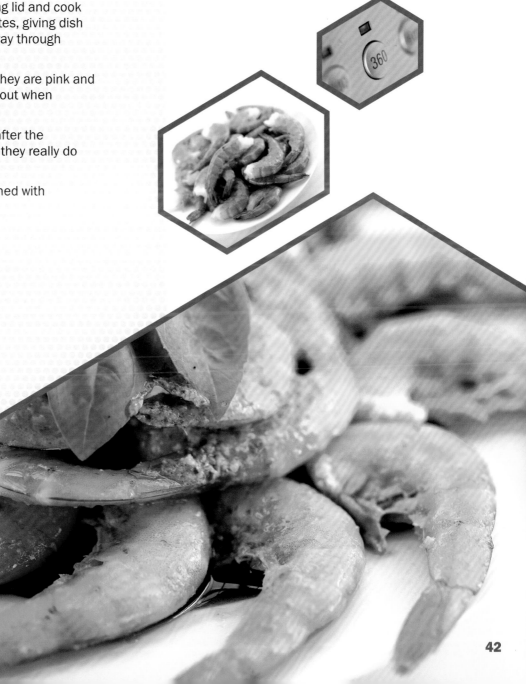

42

eggs and cheese

Eggs and cheese are often referred to as the most versatile of all foods, as they form the basis to both sweet and savoury dishes, including starters, snacks, main courses and desserts. They are, however, two foods that do require special care when cooking, especially in a microwave oven.

eggs

When microwaving, eggs should never be cooked in their shells, as steam builds up under the shell creating pressure which causes the whole egg to explode. (An exercise you will only ever do once after seeing the mess it makes in the oven!)

When white and yolk are beaten together, as in scrambled egg, a HIGH power setting can be used to achieve fluffy results. However the egg cooks very quickly and needs to be stirred or beaten every 30 seconds to ensure it does not over cook. So, as one minute passes by very quickly and the next thing you hear is 'ping!', it might be too late to rescue the eggs from turning to rubber. A MEDIUM HIGH or even MEDIUM power setting at one minute intervals will allow that

little bit more time to distribute the heat. Allow time to stir to give perfect results.

When white and yolk remain separate throughout any cooking procedure, always use a MEDIUM power setting to ensure that over-cooking, curdling or toughening does not occur.

Always pierce the yolks when cooking whole eggs to prevent them from bursting.

Where possible, always use eggs that are at room temperature. This not only speeds up the cooking process, but helps with even cooking throughout.

Remember, eggs, like all foods cooked in a microwave oven, continue to cook slightly on removal from the oven. (Especially the yolks as they retain heat.) Allow a reasonable standing time, then if still not cooked enough, continue cooking for 30 seconds at a time. Remember you can always add a little more cooking time, but an over cooked dish is ruined.

When buying eggs, always ensure the one's you choose are stamped with the 'lion mark'. This means the chickens have been innoculated against Salmonella.

cheese

Cheese melts and cooks quickly especially if grated, so it is always better to add towards the end of the cooking time. If it is just used as a topping to finish a dish, cheese always looks and smells more appetising if it is browned under a hot grill prior to serving.

Cheese dishes like rarebits and fondues cook perfectly in the microwave oven. They require less attention and stirring than if cooked conventionally, as there is no direct heat source. But, instead of burning, these dishes can over-cook and become very stringy if not watched and stirred carefully. (Very fresh, soft or processed cheese is less apt to become stringy than hard cheese).

If cooking quiches in the microwave oven, cook the pastry case first. Reduce liquid for the filling by one third. Heat and stir the egg mixture until slightly set before pouring it into the shell. This helps the filling to cook smoothly and set quickly.

tomato soufflés

serves 4

preparation time 15 minutes

Great to use up all those big beef tomatoes grown in the summer for a brunch dish, or prepare the tomatoes the day before and assemble at the last minute for a really quick impressive starter. Use a traditional English cheese as well, to bring out all the flavours, but note that all the soufflé mixture will not fit into the tomato cases, so spoon left over mixture into a shallow greased oven-proof dish and cook on MEDIUM for 5 minutes until set. Serve sliced in lettuce leaves with the tomatoes.

Cut the top off the tomatoes and reserve. Carefully scoop out the pulp and set aside. Invert the tomatoes to drain.

Meanwhile, stir together the butter, flour, milk and seasoning in a 500ml oven-proof jug. Heat on HIGH for 3 - 4 minutes, stirring every 1 minute, until the sauce comes to the boil and thickens. Stir in the cheese, thyme, reserved tomato pulp and the egg yolks.

Beat the egg whites together in a large bowl until dry and peaks form. Fold egg whites into the sauce mixture gently.

Carefully spoon the mixture into the tomato cases. Place on a flat round plate, finish with a sprinkle of grated parmesan cheese and cook on MEDIUM for 7 - 8 minutes, until the surface of the soufflé is just set but still slightly moist.

Serve hot or cold, with tomato tops as lids.

ingredients

- 4 medium or large tomatoes
- 25g butter
- 25g plain flour
- 150ml milk
- pepper to taste
- 50g Wensleydale, Derby or Lancashire cheese, grated or crumbled
- $\frac{1}{4}$ teaspn dried thyme or 1 dstspn fresh thyme, roughly chopped
- 1 tblespn fresh chopped parsley
- 3 eggs, separated
- a little grated parmesan cheese for the top

tuna and herb roll

For a dish that looks so impressive it's hard to believe that it is well within one's midweek budget to make, let alone taking only 15 minutes or so to prepare.
Try using canned salmon instead of tuna for a bit of variety.

Firstly, grease and line a shallow oblong oven-proof dish approximately 27 x 22cm with greaseproof paper. Set aside.

Put the butter, flour and milk into a 500ml oven-proof jug, heat on HIGH for 3 - 4 minutes, stirring after every 1 minute, until sauce boils and thickens.

Stir in the 3 tablespoons of dill, egg yolks and the cheese.

Beat the egg whites in a separate bowl until dry and they form soft peaks. Carefully fold into the sauce mixture. Pour mixture into the prepared dish and cook on MEDIUM HIGH for 4 - 5 minutes until top feels set to touch.

While the roll is cooking, mix tuna, onions, tomato puree, sour cream or fromage frais and lemon juice together.

Cover a large piece of greaseproof paper with the extra dill. Quickly turn the roll out on to the greaseproof paper, then cover with the tuna. Using the greaseproof paper as a guide, gently roll up like a Swiss roll.

Serve hot or cold with a green salad or hot green vegetables.

serves 4

preparation time 15 minutes

ingredients

roll:

- 25g butter
- 25g plain flour
- 250ml milk
- 3 tblspns fresh chopped dill
  plus 2 extra tblspns for garnish
- 4 eggs, separated
- 75g Double Gloucester or
  Leicester cheese, grated

filling:

- 210g can tuna drained and flaked
- 2 spring onions, chopped
- 1 tblspn tomato puree
- 3 tblspns sour cream or fromage frais
- 2 teaspns lemon juice

45

crustless asparagus quiche

This is another lovely recipe that is both quick and simple to make. The flour and soup mix settle to the base to form a pie crust, while the filling remains moist. It's also great cold - especially as part of a picnic in summer.
Use a 340g can drained asparagus spears when fresh asparagus is out of season.

Wash and trim asparagus spears and place in a shallow oven-proof dish. Cover with a well fitting lid or cling wrap and cook on HIGH for 2 minutes to part cook. Set aside while other ingredients are being prepared.

Beat the eggs, soup mix, milk and flour together in a small bowl. Stir in the cheese and spring onions. Pour mixture into a well greased 20 - 23cm oven-proof flan or quiche dish.

Arrange asparagus spears on top. Cook on HIGH for 3 minutes, then reduce power and continue cooking on MEDIUM for 15 minutes, until the mixture sets.

Cover dish with a dinner plate and leave to stand for 3 - 4 minutes before serving.

serves 4
preparation time 10 minutes

ingredients

- 200g asparagus spears, trimmed
- 4 eggs
- 45g packet dry spring vegetable soup mix
- 250ml milk
- 50g wholemeal flour
- 125g cheddar cheese, grated
- 4 spring onions roughly chopped

vegetarian

There are many reasons why people choose to eat vegetarian. Compassion for animals and religion are two important considerations, but these days, cost and variety of diet come up as equally important reasons.

Vegans (those who choose not to eat meat or fish products, including eggs, milk and cheese) and Lacto-vegetarians (those who choose not to eat meat and fish), vary their diet and obtain all the necessary nutrients through vegetables, pulses, pasta and rice so as to include all the essential proteins, minerals and vitamins.

As these form a considerable part of a vegetarian diet, they are included in this chapter. Pulses, rice and pasta are dry foods, and consequently need time to re-hydrate, so there is no time saved in cooking them in a microwave oven. However, if cooking time is accurate, they

will not boil over or stick to the cooking container, so the results are always excellent.

Rice, pasta and pulses also freeze, thaw, and re-heat well. So cook in bulk, 50g takes as long to cook as 225g. Freeze any left overs as soon as it goes cold. Thaw on MEDIUM LOW and re-heat on MEDIUM HIGH stirring occasionally to even out heat distribution and separate grains and pieces.

All pulses except lentils require an overnight soaking to soften them before cooking; then, before using, rinse thoroughly under cold running water. Place in a large, deep, oven-proof dish; cover generously with boiling water or stock, bring liquid back to the boil using a HIGH power setting (to kill any harmful toxins), then complete the cooking time on MEDIUM. Pasta may be cooked in the microwave oven while the accompanying sauce is cooked

on the hob or vice-versa. Cooking pasta is the same as for pulses - bring water or stock to the boil, add pasta, stir well. Reduce power to MEDIUM then follow pack instructions for cooking times.

Rice, cooked by the absorption method cooks and fluffs up beautifully. Place 225g of well washed long grain rice into a large deep oven-proof dish. Pour over 450ml of boiling water or stock, stir well. Cook on HIGH for 10 minutes, stir again, then complete the cooking time on MEDIUM. Read the pack instructions as different varieties require different cooking times. When completed, leave to stand, covered for 2 - 3 minutes, then just before serving fluff up with a fork. I use 1 cup of rice and 2 cups of boiling liquid for 2 people - that way I don't have to get the scales out!

carrot and parsnip loaf

I love the colour of this dish, and even though I am definitely not a vegetarian I love the flavour. It also goes very well served with a tomato based pasta sauce and is great as an accompaniment to roasts. I even serve it cold with salad.

Place carrots, parsnips, water, garlic and butter in a large oven-proof dish. Cover with a well fitting lid and cook on HIGH for 10 minutes until vegetables are tender. Stir, or give the dish a good shake half way through cooking time. Leave to stand for a few minutes.

For a smooth loaf, put vegetable mixture into a food processor and purée until smooth. For a coarser loaf, or if a processor is not to hand, mash with a potato masher.

Stir in eggs, cheese and seasoning to taste. Pour mixture into a greased oven-proof loaf or ring dish. Level off top and cook on MEDIUM HIGH for 10 - 13 minutes, until mixture is set and a sharp knife inserted into the centre of the loaf comes out clean. Allow loaf to stand, covered for 5 minutes, before turning out on to serving plate.

serves 4 - 6

preparation time 15 minutes

ingredients

- 450g carrots, peeled and finely chopped or sliced
- 375g parsnips, peeled and finely chopped or sliced
- 75ml water
- 1 clove garlic, crushed
- 50g butter
- 3 eggs, beaten
- 125g Emmenthal cheese, grated
- 1 teaspn prepared mustard
- seasoning to taste
- few fresh coriander leaves for garnish

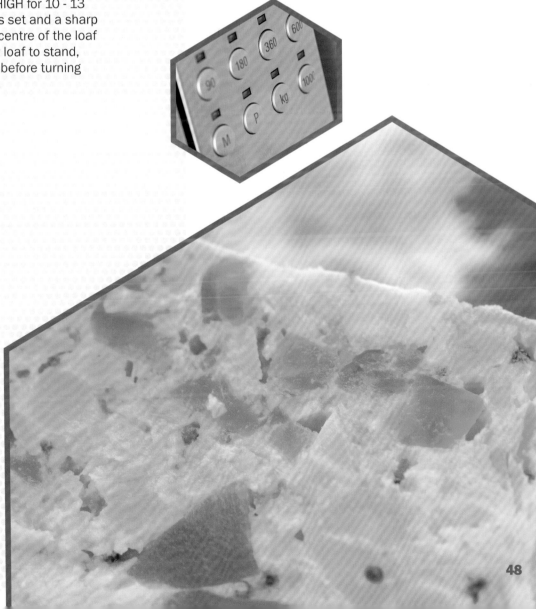

48

spicy chickpeas and rice

Serve this great vegetarian dish with a tomato salad and cucumber and mint tzatziki. You can even cook the accompanying poppadums in the microwave oven.
Place 3 poppadums on the turntable at a time, but do not allow them to overlap. Cook on MEDIUM HIGH for 45 seconds until light. Remember they will not have changed colour but will crisp as they cool.

Put the butter and onion into an oven-proof dish, cover with a well fitting lid and cook on HIGH for 2 minutes until soft. Stir in the spices and curry paste. Return to the oven and continue to cook on MEDIUM HIGH for 1 minute. Stir in the rice, lemon rind and juice, tomato puree and boiling vegetable stock. Cook uncovered on HIGH for 8 minutes.

Stir in the chickpeas and continue to cook, uncovered, on MEDIUM for 5 - 8 minutes until all stock has been absorbed and the rice is thoroughly cooked. If necessary, add a little more boiling water if all the liquid has been absorbed before the rice is thoroughly cooked. Cover dish, leave to stand for 3 - 4 minutes, Adjust seasonings to taste and serve sprinkled with the chopped nuts.

serves 2 - 3

preparation time 5 minutes

ingredients

- 25g butter
- 1 onion, sliced
- $\frac{1}{2}$ teaspn ground cumin
- $\frac{1}{2}$ teaspn ground coriander
- 1 teaspn curry paste
- 125g brown or a mixture of white and wild rice, well washed
- finely grated rind and juice of 1 lemon
- 1 tblspn tomato puree
- 450ml boiling vegetable stock
- 210g can chickpeas, rinsed and drained
- black pepper to taste
- 25g nuts, e.g. peanuts, cashews, roughly chopped

mushroom tagliatelle

A meal the kids can prepare. It's also quick, nutritious, filling, and well within budget. Use cubes of feta cheese instead of ricotta for a stronger flavoured dish.

Cook tagliatelle in a large saucepan of boiling, salted water on top of the stove for 10 - 12 minutes until tender. Drain well and set aside.

While pasta is cooking, put butter into a 1 - 2 litre ovenproof dish or casserole and cook on HIGH for 1 minute until melted and starting to bubble. Stir in spring onions, peppers and mushrooms. Mix well and cook on HIGH for 3 - 4 minutes until softened together. Stir in ricotta cheese, parmesan and seasonings.
Re-cover and continue to cook on MEDIUM for 5 minutes until well blended; stir half way through the cooking time.

Adjust seasonings to taste.

Fold the mushroom mixture through the hot, drained pasta together with the cream.

Serve hot, garnished with parsley.

serves 4

preparation time 15 minutes

ingredients

- 375g pack tagliatelle - use tomato or spinach for extra colour
- 25g butter
- 6 spring onions, finely chopped
- 1 red pepper, de-seeded and sliced
- 1 green pepper, de-seeded and sliced
- 200g mushrooms, wiped and sliced
- 150g Ricotta cheese
- 100g grated Parmesan cheese
- $^1/_4$ - $^1/_2$ teaspn cayenne pepper
- few drops of tabasco sauce (optional)
- fresh ground black pepper to taste
- 75ml single cream
- parsley to garnish

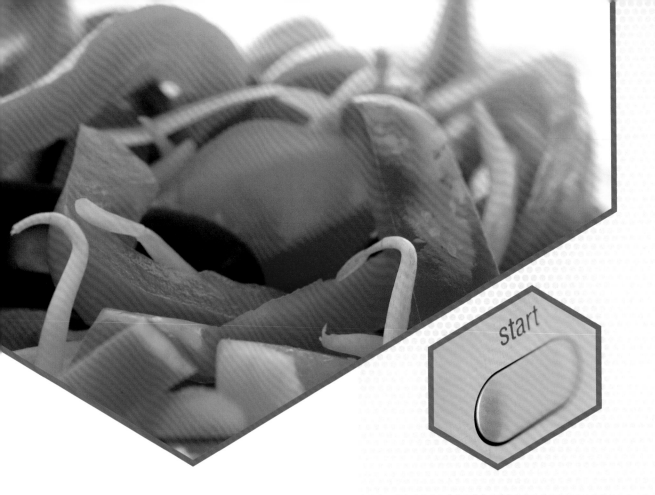

start

vegetables

I can honestly say the adage 'Beautiful things happen to vegetables when they are cooked in a microwave oven' is true.

Their colour and flavour is enhanced and they retain more of their natural nutrients than by any other cooking method - so they are much better for you to eat - and you don't have to eat as much to get the same nutrients as if they were cooked conventionally.

But here are a few points to remember in order to cook them to perfection:

On average, 1 portion of vegetables for 1 person, cooked covered on a dinner plate or in a small microwave proof cooking dish, will take 2 minutes to cook in a 900 watt oven. 2 portions put on the same plate or in the same dish will take 3 minutes to cook. 3 portions will take $3\frac{1}{2}$ - 4 minutes to cook, plus 1 - 2 minutes of standing time. 4 portions of vegetables for 1

person will take approximately 5 minutes to cook. However, because every oven varies, try cooking your first batch of 4 vegetables for one person for 4 minutes. Leave to stand for 1 minute, then test for doneness - to your own taste. If not cooked enough, return to the oven and continue to cook for a further 1 minute at a time. When cooked to your satisfaction, use that cooking time as your bench mark for future cooking. Remember to always undercook until you have worked out your own ideal cooking times. Over-cooked vegetables are ruined.

You can see from this that for each additional vegetable the cooking time is not quite doubled.

Remember, use a minimum amount of water for the cooking process. You are cooking vegetables, not boiling water! Wash and/or peel the vegetables, then cut into uniform sizes - the smaller they are, the quicker

they will cook. Put into a sealable plastic microwave cook bag or oven-proof dish that has a well fitting lid. Cook in only the water that adheres to the vegetables, they will 'steam' in their own natural moisture.

Always keep the dish covered during cooking, as this holds in the steam, shortens the cooking time and prevents the contents from drying out. If the dish does not have a well fitting lid, use cling film to cover or a large microwaveable dinner plate, but do not let cling film touch the food.

Prick vegetables that are cooked in their skins (e.g. potatoes, tomatoes and squash) all over with a fork prior to cooking, to prevent the skins from bursting, and allow the steam to escape.

Never add salt before cooking. Salt acts as a dielectric and leaches the moisture out of the food, making it dry and woody. Try eating vegetables without salt. - You will find that as they have been cooked in a microwave oven they are much more flavourful anyway - so maybe you won't want the salt. But if you must add it, sprinkle sparingly over to taste after the cooking process has been completed.

Quantity and size affect the whole cooking process. A whole carrot or head of cauliflower will take much longer to cook than a vegetable that has been divided into small evenly sized pieces.

One medium sized potato to be baked in its jacket will take approximately 3 - 4 minutes to cook on HIGH power. Four potatoes don't take 4 times as long to cook, but do take a proportionately longer time - in this case 10 - 12 minutes.

Try to arrange halved or whole vegetables like carrot sticks or potato wedges in a ring around the outer edge of the dish, leaving the centre clear and space between the foods. Place tender ends of asparagus or broccoli towards the centre of the oven, so that the stalks cook slightly more that the centre. Standing time is almost as important as the cooking itself, as this allows time for the heat to penetrate through larger vegetables to cook and tenderise the centre, without overcooking the outer edges. Food should always be covered during standing to hold in the heat generated.

Remember always cook food for the minimum cooking time. You can always 'add' a little extra cooking time, but over cooked vegetables are ruined, because all the natural moisture in the food has been driven off in the form of steam. Then all you are left with is dry, tough, inedible fibres.

So, learn from the mistakes of others. Undercook first, add extra cooking time, a little at a time, and use that cooking time for perfect results in the future.

Last but not least, if you live on your own, freshly cooked vegetables need never be a problem. Cook them directly on the dinner plate or simply in a plastic cook bag. For example, put a few sprigs of washed broccoli and 1 small peeled and quartered, washed potato on the plate first. Cover the plate with cling wrap or place in a cook bag, seal the bag and cook on HIGH for 2 minutes. Add 1 carrot, sliced into sticks and continue to cook, well sealed, for a further 2 minutes. Lastly add 2 tablespoons of frozen peas, re-seal and cook for a further 2 minutes. Allow to stand for 2 minutes before serving - and there you are! Lovely freshly cooked vegetables, eaten from one warm dinner plate and only one piece of washing up to do afterwards!

vegetable cooking chart

Vegetable	Fresh or frozen	Amount	Method of cooking	Cooking time on high (mins)	Serving suggestions
Artichoke	Fresh	1 medium 3 medium	Wrap in cling film wrap wrap separately as above	2 - 3 6 - 7	Serve cold with French dressing
Asparagus	fresh	500g	Wash carefully, place in a shallow oven proof dish, cover dish with a plate or cling wrap, shake or move half way through cooking	3 - 4	Serve hot with melted butter or cold with French dressing or Hollandaise sauce. Don't over-cook
Beans - French whole	fresh	500g	Place in a shallow oven-proof dish cover with cling wrap or well fitting lid	6 - 8	Serve hot, buttered or sprinkled with toasted almonds
Beans - French sliced	fresh	500g	Cook as above	5 - 7	
Beans - French	frozen	1 portion	In a small covered dish	3	with a knob of butter
Beans - broad	fresh	1 portion	cook as above	2 - 3	
Beans - broad	frozen	1 portion	cook as above	2 - 3	
Beans - broad	frozen	225g	In plastic cook-bag or oven-proof dish, covered	4 - 5	
Beetroot	fresh, unpeeled	500g (4 medium)	In a small covered dish	10 - 12	peeled, hot as a vegetable or cold as a salad accompanyment
Broccoli	fresh	500g, divided into florets	In a plastic cook-bag or oven-proof dish, covered	5 - 6	buttered or garnished with chopped hard boiled egg
	frozen	225g	cook as above	4 - 5	
Brussels Sprouts	fresh	500g	In a plastic cook-bag or oven-proof dish, covered - score base with a sharp knife	5 - 6	with a knob of butter
	frozen	225g	cook as above	4 - 5	
Cabbage inc. Curly Kale	fresh	1/2 medium 225g	In a plastic cook-bag or oven-proof dish, covered	5 - 6	Serve hot, buttered sprinkled with freshly ground black pepper or lemon juice
Carrots	fresh, cut into strips	225g	In a plastic cook-bag or oven-proof dish, covered	4 - 5	Serve hot, tossed with sesame seeds and drizzled with honey
	frozen	225g	cook as above	4 - 5	
Cauliflower	fresh	1 whole divided into florets	In a plastic cook-bag or oven-proof dish, covered	5 - 6	Serve hot with parsley or cheese sauce then browned under a hot grill
	frozen	225g	cook as above	5 - 6	
Celery	fresh	2 sticks	Cut into 10cm sticks, cook in a plastic cook-bag or oven-proof dish, covered	1 - 2	Serve hot sprinkled with fresh mixed herbs or covered with cheese sauce and browned under a hot grill
Corn	fresh	1 cob 2 cobs	Wrap in cling wrap, put into a plastic cook bag, or in a covered oven proof dish	2 2 - 3	Serve hot, buttered
Courgettes	fresh	4 small	Slice into 2cm slices, cook in a shallow oven-proof dish, covered	2	Serve with tomato slices, or stir into a casserole, just before serving
Leeks	fresh	2 medium	Cut into 10cm strips, cook in a plastic cook-bag or oven-proof dish, covered	2 - 3	Serve with white or cheese sauce,
Mushrooms	fresh	250g	Well washed, trim stalks, cook in a single layer in a shallow oven-proof dish, covered	2 - do not over-cook	Serve on top of grilled meat or stirred into a casserole before serving

vegetable cooking chart

Vegetable	Fresh or frozen	Amount	Method of cooking	Cooking time on high (mins)	Serving suggestions
Onions	fresh	2 large quartered	Cook in a shallow oven-proof dish, covered or as a basis for casseroles	2 - 3	Serve with grilled meats, or stirred into a casserole before serving
Parsnips	fresh	2 medium	Cut into quarters, cook in a plastic cook- bag or oven-proof dish, covered	4 - 5	Half cook, then roast until crisp, serve drizzled with a little honey
Peas	fresh	1 portion	In a plastic cook-bag or oven-proof dish, covered	2	Do not over cook, serve hot, buttered, garnished with fresh mint leaves
	frozen	1 portion	cook as above	2	
Potatoes	fresh - jacket	1 medium	Prick all over with a fork, cook straight on oven rack, one in centre, 2 side by side, 3 in a triangle, 4 in a square	4	Serve split and filled with butter, soured cream, grated cheese, chilli, baked beans or coleslaw
		2 medium		5 - 6	
		4 medium		11 - 13	
	fresh - peeled	2 medium	Cut into small evenly sized pieces	5 - 6	Serve hot with roast meat, mashed, or part-cooked then roasted in a hot oven
		500g	Cook in a shallow, covered, oven-proof dish	8 - 10	
Sweet Potatoes	fresh	1 - 300g	Prick all over with a fork, cook straight on oven rack, one in centre, 2 side by side, 3 in a triangle	3 - 4	Serve hot, creamed with meat and fish
		2 - 600g		5 - 6	
		3 - 1kg		10 - 12	
Peppers	fresh	1 whole	Cut in half, place on glass plate	1	Peel skin, use in curries, stews etc, great for extra flavour
Pumpkin/ Squash	fresh	375g	Peel, cut into chunks, cook in an oven-proof dish, covered	6 - 8	Serve with a knob of butter and sprinkling of black pepper, creamed with potato or part cooked then roasted with potatoes
Snow peas (Mange Tout)	fresh	500g	In a plastic cook bag or oven-proof dish, covered	4 - 5	Serve with baby corn and sprinkled with sesame seeds
	frozen	500g	Cook as above	5 - 6	
Spinach	fresh	375g	Cook in a plastic cook-bag or small oven-proof dish, with only the water that adheres to its leaves. Well covered, shake dish during cooking	3 - 4	Serve as a base for eggs florentine, quiche or a vegetable accompanyment
	frozen	375g	Cook as above, icy side upwards	6 - 8	
Swede	fresh	225g	Peel, cut into 1cm cubes, wash, cook in a plastic cook-bag or oven-proof dish, covered. Shake half way through cooking time	4 - 6	Serve with roasts, or mashed with carrots or added to stews for extra flavour
	frozen	225g		4 - 6	
Tomatoes	fresh	2 whole, large	Halve tomatoes cross wise, place on a paper towel	2 - 3	Serve as a snack or vegetable accompanyment, topped with grated cheese
Turnip	fresh	225g	Peel, cut into 1cm cubes, wash, cook in a plastic cook-bag or oven-proof dish, covered. Shake halfway through cooking time	5 - 7	Serve with roasts, season liberally with pepper and thyme before serving
Vegetables - Mixed - chunky	frozen	225g	cook in a plastic cook-bag or oven-proof dish, stir or shake dish half way through cooking time	6 - 8	
Mixed - small	frozen	225g		5 - 6	

serves 3 - 4

preparation time a few minutes
if using frozen vegetables,
10 - 15 minutes if preparing
vegetables from scratch

ingredients

- 500g mixed vegetables, e.g. sliced
  red, green and/or yellow peppers,
  carrots, cut into sticks, chopped
  celery, sliced onion or spring onions,
  bean sprouts, trimmed snow peas
  and/or baby sweet corn
- 210g can water chestnuts,
  drained and sliced
- 2 tblspns green ginger wine
- 2 tblspns Chinese plum sauce

quick stir-fry chinese vegetables

The vegetables take longer to cut up and prepare than the whole dish takes to cook, so if you're really short of time use frozen ready prepared ones, but be careful not to over cook, as frozen vegetables have been par-cooked prior to being frozen. They should still be crunchy to taste.

Put washed and prepared vegetables into a large oven-proof dish, add the ginger wine, cover with a well fitting lid and cook on HIGH for 6 - 8 minutes, giving dish a good shake or stir half way cooking time.

Stir through plum sauce and serve immediately with rice.

serves 3 - 4

preparation time 5 - 10 minutes-
according to how dirty the leeks are

ingredients

- 6 medium sized leeks
- 1 tblspn fresh chopped tarragon
  or 1 teaspn dried tarragon
- 1 tblspn roughly chopped parsley
- small pinch thyme
- 1 tblspn lemon juice
- 2 tblspns water
- black pepper to taste
- 1 tomato, skinned and sliced

herbed leeks

**Another example of how the microwave enhances not only the flavour of vegetables but the colour as well.
No nutrients are lost during this cooking process, so enjoy this symphony of flavours!**

Trim the leeks, leaving 5 cm of green top. Cut diagonally through leaves to within 6cm of the bulb end, spread leaves slightly and thoroughly wash to remove any grit.

Place leeks in a shallow oven-proof dish, sprinkle with the herbs, lemon juice, water and black pepper to taste.

Cover dish with a well fitting lid or cling wrap and cook on HIGH for 3 minutes. Turn leeks over in dish, arrange slices of tomato on top. Continue cooking on HIGH for 2 - 3 minutes until slightly tender when tested with a sharp knife.

Leave covered in dish for 2 - 3 minutes before serving.

stuffed aubergines

Vegetarians might like to omit the minced beef from this recipe and substitute it with diced tofu or quorn pieces for a good substantial main course meal. The cooking time remains the same.

Cut aubergines in half. Scoop out centre and roughly chop. Set aside. Rinse aubergines under running water, then leave to soak in cold watrer until required.

Place the butter, pinenuts and onion in a 1 litre oven-proof dish. Cover with a well fitting lid or cling wrap and cook on HIGH for 2 minutes. Stir in beef mince, breadcrumbs or rice, spices, herbs and reserved chopped aubergine. Re-cover dish and continue cooking on MEDIUM HIGH for 5 minutes, stirring well after 2 minutes until meat is cooked and has lost it's pink colour. Adjust seasonings to taste.

Drain aubergines, set 2 halves in a shallow oven-proof dish. Fill each with stuffing mixture. Top with remaining aubergine halves.

Cover dish with a well fitting lid or cling wrap and cook on MEDIUM for 10 minutes until aubergine is tender and feels soft when pricked with a fork and filling is piping hot throughout.

Leave covered to stand for 2 minutes. Set on a serving plate, pour yogurt over, then sprinkle with reserved mint.

serves 4 as a vegetable accompaniment or 2 as a main course

preparation time 15 minutes

ingredients

- 2 aubergines
- 25g butter
- 2 tblspns pinenuts
- 1 large onion, chopped
- 250g fresh beef mince
- 2 tblspns fresh breadcrumbs or
- 2 tblspns cook long grain rice
- $1/2$ teaspn mixed spice
- $1/2$ teaspn mixed herbs
- black pepper and salt to taste
- 200g carton natural yogurt
- 2 tblspns fresh mint, roughly chopped

56

courgettes with chilli and mint

A very nice unusual blend of exotic flavours here, ideal for those looking for something a little different to do with home grown courgettes.

Cut the courgettes into thick matchsticks (approximately 1 - 2 cm wide by 6 - 8 cm long). Rinse under cold running water, then leave to soak in cold water while other ingredients are being prepared. Drain and put into a medium sized oven-proof dish, add chopped garlic cloves, mint leaves, chilli sauce and wine vinegar. Stir well to distribute spices.

Cover dish with a well fitting lid or cling wrap and cook on HIGH for 3 - 4 minutes until tender. Remove mint leaves and serve immediately.

serves 3 - 4
preparation time 5 minutes

ingredients

- 450g courgettes
- 2 cloves garlic, finely chopped
  handful of fresh mint leaves
- 2 teaspns chilli sauce
- 1 tblspn red wine vinegar

sweet and sour red cabbage

Great with barbecued meats and burgers.

Place all ingredients in a large oven-proof dish. Cover with a well fitting lid or cling wrap and cook on HIGH for 3 minutes. Stir or give dish a good shake to re-distribute ingredients, re-cover and continue cooking on HIGH for a further 3 minutes until cooked through, but still slightly crisp to bite.

Allow to stand, covered, for 2 - 3 minutes before serving.

serves 3 - 4
preparation time 5 - 10 minutes

ingredients

- $1/2$ small red cabbage, washed and finely sliced
- 3 - 4 water chestnuts, sliced
- 1 green apple, washed and diced
- 1 onion, finely chopped
- 2 rings canned pineapple, chopped
- 2 tblspns pineapple juice from can
- 3 tblspns wine vinegar

spaghetti squash with tomato sauce

Spaghetti squash is one of those vegetables that is usually very difficult to cook, so it's not bought very often. But, now is the opportunity to try it, as it is a truly great summer vegetable and cooks perfectly in the microwave oven. Simply pierce the skin all over with a sharp knife or skewer and cook on HIGH for 10 - 15 minutes according to size. It is cooked when a sharp knife goes easily through flesh to the centre. Carefully cut in half (but be aware, it will be hot!) Remove seeds and fork-up strands. Serve with melted butter or this delicious sauce, for a great vegetarian meal or accompaniment to any meat dish.

This sauce recipe makes approximately 1 litre, so use some to accompany this dish and freeze some for later.

Cook squash first, according to instructions above. While cooking, prepare vegetables for sauce. When squash is cooked, before cutting set on a serving plate and cover with foil to keep warm and complete it's cooking time.

Place oil, onions and garlic in an oven-proof dish or casserole. Cover with a well fitting lid or cling wrap and cook on HIGH for 2 minutes. Stir in tomatoes, re-cover dish and continue to cook on HIGH for a further 2 minutes. Stir in tomato paste, oregano, basil and pepper to taste. Cook on HIGH for 5 - 6 minutes, stirring occasionally until tomatoes are thoroughly cooked.

Cut squash in half, tease strands of 'spaghetti' with a fork onto warm serving plate or dish. Top with tomato sauce. Serve immediately.

serves 2 - 4 according to size of squash

preparation time 10 minutes at most

ingredients

- 1 large spaghetti squash

tomato sauce:

- 2 tblspns olive oil
- 2 onions, finely chopped
- 1 clove garlic, finely chopped or crushed
- 1 kg ripe tomatoes, peeled and roughly chopped
- 85g can tomato paste
- 2 tblspns fresh chopped oregano
- 2 tblspns fresh chopped basil
- black pepper to taste

58

sauces

Making a sauce in the microwave oven is a great confidence builder, as perfect results are almost guaranteed. So, if making a lump-free white sauce or even custard in a saucepan on top of the stove still eludes you, try some of these recipes.

By watching, frequent stirring, making use of the residual heat and, most importantly, the standing time that completes the cooking procedure, great sauces can be prepared quickly and safely.

The reason for this is that there is no direct heat, so the base cannot burn or over-cook, the sauce doesn't stick to the sides and base of the pan, and, of course, the cooking time is left to you. If distracted or the phone rings, turn the oven off and answer the call. The sauce will not ruin - it will be in the same stage of preparation as when it was left.

Sauces cooked in the microwave oven also take less time to cook than conventionally, they don't need continuous stirring or watching as the heat is coming in from all sides. However it is essential to stir every 1 minute, so put the oven on for 1 minute spurts to give the best lump free results.

Even the classic egg yolk based sauces work like a dream. They cook in moments. The answer to their success is 'don't leave the oven'! Open the door and whisk or stir at every opportunity - at the sight of a bubble, open the door and stir, every 10 seconds if needs be. The sauce will take less than 2 minutes to cook at the most, and it thickens before your eyes. Don't forget too that the heat is in the food, so it will continue cooking slightly on removal from the oven.

Basic white sauces, custards and gravies can be cooked on HIGH power. Sauces that contain eggs and/or cheese need to be cooked on a lower setting, like MEDIUM to prevent them boiling over or over-cooking. Stirred custards if under-cooked will be thin, but, if over-cooked, will curdle.

For those intolerant of wheat flour, substitute 15g of cornflour for 25g ordinary flour in sauces. The flavour and results will be the same.

It is best to cook 500ml of sauce in a 1 - 2 litre container. This gives room for the sauce to expand, a greater surface area for even and shorter cooking time, and room for stirring.

So, cook and enjoy a fabulous Bearnaise sauce with a grilled steak, Hollandaise with asparagus or salmon, chocolate sauce with a steamed sponge or Brandy sauce with Christmas pudding. You will amaze yourself at just how clever you are. Suddenly, making sauces becomes simple!

the basic savoury sauce

Place all ingredients into a 1 litre oven-proof dish or jug. Stir well to distribute the flour and heat on HIGH for 1 minute. Remove from the oven and stir again to continue to distribute the flour and blend it in with the melting butter and heating milk.

Return jug to the oven and continue heating on HIGH for 3 - 4 minutes, stirring well after every minute, until the sauce boils and thickens.

Using this cooking method no lumps can form, and none of the mixture sticks to the sides or base of the dish. The golden rule with all sauces is to stir often to prevent lumps forming and ensure a smooth glossy result.

Variations:

Cheese: Stir in 50 - 75g grated cheese to the basic sauce at the end of the cooking time. Use to pour over cooked cauliflower. Sprinkle with a little extra grated cheese, put under a hot grill or into a hot oven for 3 - 5 minutes to brown the top.

Mustard: Sounds old fashioned, but honestly, taste this with a gammon steak or over some broccoli - it's lovely! Just stir 2 teaspoons of prepared French mustard, 2 teaspoons of prepared horseradish cream and $1/2$ teaspoon Worcestershire sauce into the basic sauce.

Bread Sauce: Believe me, it's more complicated making up a packet bread sauce than it is to make it from scratch. Just stir 25g fresh white bread crumbs into the basic sauce mixture and leave to stand for 15 minutes, adjust seasonings to taste before serving. You might want to add some salt.

Curry Sauce: Stir 2 teaspoons of curry powder and 1 teaspoon of prepared horseradish cream into completed basic sauce.

makes 250ml

preparation time 5 minutes

ingredients

- 25g butter
- 25g plain flour
- 250ml milk
- pinch black pepper
- large pinch dry mustard powder or 1 teaspn prepared grainy mustard

60

classic hollandaise and bearnaise sauce

You CAN make this sauce! Just remember that the egg yolks will curdle if the sauce is over-cooked, and as it does cook so quickly, keep watching, opening the oven door and whisking as often as possible. If the sauce does begin to separate, add a few drops of boiling water and whisk until it becomes smooth again, but don't cook it for any longer. It will keep for up to 1 week refrigerated in a sealed container.

Put the lemon juice, vinegar, peppercorns and bay leaf into a $^1/_2$ litre oven-proof bowl or jug. Heat, uncovered, on HIGH for 1 minute until the liquid boils. Continue cooking on HIGH for a further 2 minutes until the liquid has reduced by half.

Strain this mixture into a clean $^1/_2$ litre ovenproof bowl or jug. Add the butter pieces and heat on HIGH for 15 - 30 seconds, or until the butter melts.

In a separate $^1/_2$ litre oven-proof bowl, whisk the egg yolks well. Add the hot melted butter mixture slowly in a gradual stream, whisking continuously until all ingredients are well combined. Cook the sauce on MEDIUM for 30 - 60 seconds, whisking every 15 seconds, until the sauce thickens slightly.
Continue whisking, until sauce is smooth and glossy. Leave to stand for 2 - 3 minutes. The sauce will thicken slightly on standing. Adjust seasonings to taste, adding a little more lemon juice if desired for a more piquant flavour.

Bearnaise Sauce is made in the same way as Hollandaise, just substitute the lemon juice for 3 tablespoons of wine vinegar, add a slice of onion and pinch of tarragon to the boiling vinegar mixture and stir in a teaspoon of fresh chopped parsley at the end.

makes 100ml

preparation time 10 minutes

ingredients

- 1 tblspn lemon juice
- 1 tblspn white wine vinegar
- 4 peppercorns
- 1 bay leaf
- 125g butter cut into small pieces
- yolks of 2 large eggs, beaten
- seasoning to taste
- pinch dry mustard if desired
- black pepper to taste

basic sweet sauces

custard

Blend together 1 tablespoon custard powder, 1 tablespoon sugar and a little milk taken from 250ml, in a $^1/_2$ litre oven-proof jug. When mixture forms a smooth paste, stir in remaining milk. Cook on HIGH for 3 - 4 minutes, stirring every 1 minute until milk boils and sauce thickens.

brandy

Blend together 1 tablespoon cornflour, 2 tablespoons sugar with a little milk taken from 250mls, in a $^1/_2$ litre oven-proof jug. When mixture forms a smooth paste, stir in remaining milk and 1 teaspoon butter. Cook on HIGH power for 3 - 4 minutes, stirring every 1 minute until milk boils and sauce thickens. Stir in 3 tablespoons brandy. Serve hot.

almond

Omit the brandy, but stir 1 teaspoon almond extract in with the milk at the beginning of the cooking time. This is great served with fruit based winter puddings.

chocolate

Stir 1 tablespoon cocoa powder, 2 tablespoons sugar and 1 tablespoon cornflour together with a little of the 250ml milk until a smooth paste is formed. Stir in remaining milk and cook as above.

orange and lemon

Omit the brandy and stir in1 tablespoon lemon and 1 tablespoon orange juice at the end of the cooking time when the sauce has stopped bubbling.

desserts

No matter whether they are light or heavy, all types of desserts and family puddings cook well in a microwave oven, and of course they are cooked in a fraction of the time taken conventionally.

here are a few simple tips to help master the art of making the perfect pud:

Sponge, suet and Christmas type puddings cook and rise well in a microwave oven. Cover the cooking bowl with greaseproof paper (pleat it first to allow for expansion) rather than cling film, which can sometimes make sponge puddings a little soggy.

Be careful not to over-cook sponge puddings either, as due to the shape of the basin the top will cook before the base. Always allow a good standing time to distribute the heat evenly and complete the cooking time. Fruit, like vegetables, have a lovely fresh flavour and bright colour when cooked in the microwave oven. Be careful not to over-cook fruit as it softens rapidly then loses its shape. Rhubarb, or soft fruit such as blackberries do not generally need any additional water prior to stewing, just a little sugar or honey. But the addition of 2 - 3 tablespoons of water added to plums or apples helps with the cooking process. Dried fruit needs no pre-soaking prior to cooking, but it should have enough water added to allow absorption to its full capacity during the cooking and standing time.

Egg and milk based puddings cook best on a MEDIUM power level to prevent over-cooking and curdling.

Christmas pudding both cooks and re-heats most successfully in the microwave oven. A 450g pudding will take approximately 5 minutes to reheat thoroughly, but it should be done carefully as, due to it's high sugar and alcohol content, it could burn easily. It is actually better to cut the pudding into portions and reheat each portion separately, for 1 minute, to ensure it's thoroughly cooked and heated through.

Individual puddings, custards or whole fruits such as baked apples, should be set on a large oven-proof plate and arranged in a circle, keeping the centre free, so that all the foods absorb the same amount of power and cook evenly.

Pastry and meringue are best cooked conventionally. Pastry can be cooked in a microwave, but as both need to 'dry out' during the cooking process, they are best if cooked in a combination oven.

sticky toffee pudding

I love these hot steamed sponge type puddings, especially during the winter. Sticky toffee is my favourite. Serve it with the sauce poured over then add a dollop of vanilla ice cream. Cooked in just 7 - 8 minutes. What could be easier!

Heat the apple juice or water in a 500ml oven-proof jug or bowl on HIGH for 3 minutes, until steaming. Stir in the chopped dates. Set aside to soak for an hour or so.

Mix together all ingredients for sponge in a large mixing bowl, beat together until smooth. Drain dates and discard any excess liquid, stir into sponge mixture.

Pour mixture into a well greased 500ml pudding basin or round deep cooking dish. Cover with a piece of greaseproof paper and cook on MEDIUM HIGH for 7 - 8 minutes, until well risen and when a skewer or sharp knife is inserted into the centre of the sponge comes out clean.

Leave to stand. Meanwhile prepare sauce:

Put remaining butter, brown sugar and cream into an ovenproof bowl. Melt together on MEDIUM for 2 minutes, Stir well to ensure sugar is melted, then continue to cook on MEDIUM HIGH for 3 - 4 minutes, until mixture begins to bubble; stir well.

Turn pudding out of cooking basin on to a large serving plate and serve with sauce poured over.

serves 3 - 4

preparation time
15 minutes, excluding soaking time for dates

ingredients

- 150 ml apple juice or water
- 125g dates, roughly chopped
- 85g butter, softened
- 125g brown sugar
- 2 eggs
- 175g self raising flour
- 1 teaspn bicarbonate of soda
- $1/_2$ teaspn ground ginger (or to taste)
- $1/_2$ teaspn ground nutmeg (or to taste)
- $1/_2$ teaspn vanilla essence

toffee sauce:

- 125g butter
- 175g brown sugar
- 125ml single cream

almond nectarines

**Another of my great store cupboard recipes.
Use large Victoria plums instead of nectarines in summer,
or canned peach halves in winter when fresh nectarines
are not available.**

Beat together the almonds, sugar, butter and almond extract.

Place nectarine halves, cut side uppermost in a large
shallow oven-proof dish. Pile the filling mixture onto each
half. Pour fruit juice over the fruit.

Cook on HIGH for 5 - 6 minutes until filling cooks, begins to
bubble, and nectarines heat through.

If you want, place under a hot grill for 2 - 3 minutes, just
before serving to brown the tops.

Serve immediately with whipped cream or ice cream.

serves 4
preparation time 8 - 10 minutes

ingredients

- 125g ground almonds
- 125g Demerara sugar
- 50g butter
- few drops almond extract or essence
- 4 large ripe nectarines, washed and
  halved with stones removed
- 150ml fruit juice

toffee covered oranges

**There's no end to the number of elegant fruit based
desserts you can make in the microwave oven. Substitute
banana or apple slices for the oranges and serve with ice
cream for a really quick dessert.**

Prepare the fruit, set in a shallow serving dish and refrigerate
until required.

Place the sugar and boiling water into a 2 litre oven-proof
dish or jug. Stir well. Heat on HIGH for 8 - 9 minutes, stirring
well after every 2 minutes, until syrup boils and begins to
turn a golden brown colour. Remove from the oven
immediately. Stir well, it will continue to darken in colour as
you stir. Pour over oranges. Toffee will set instantly on contact
with the chilled fruit.

For a thinner sauce, instead of a set toffee covering.
Stir 100mls of warm water into syrup on removal from oven.
Be careful, though as it will bubble up quickly and will be very
hot. Stir well until water has been absorbed by the syrup.
Pour sauce over oranges. Serve cold.

serves 3 - 4
preparation time 5 - 6 minutes,
excluding boiling up the sugar syrup

ingredients

- 4 oranges, peeled and cut into
  1cm slices
- 125g caster sugar
- 125ml boiling water

ginger and pumpkin cheesecake

Please try this one! Pumpkin is used lots in different parts of the world, and quite rightly so. It is delicious; either in pumpkin pie or in this cheesecake.

Melt butter in a medium sized bowl on HIGH for 1 minute. Mix with biscuit crumbs. Press into the base of a 23cm ovenproof pie plate or loose bottomed flan case. Chill while preparing filling.

Chop pumpkin into 1 - 2 cm cubes, rinse under cold water. Put into an oven-proof bowl. Cover with a well fitting lid or cling wrap and cook on HIGH for 5 - 6 minutes until soft. Purée in a food processor or mash with a potato masher.

If using a food processor, add in ginger pieces, then soft cheese, sugar, lemon juice and rind. Blend until smooth. Lastly blend in eggs.

If puréeing pumpkin with a potato masher, mash in a large mixing bowl. Add ginger, soft cheese, sugar, rind and juice of lemon and eggs and beat until well combined.

Pour mixture over biscuit base and cook on MEDIUM for 30 - 40 minutes until set. Centre may still be a little soft, but a plate put on top of cooking dish for 5 minutes will hold in the heat, complete the cooking and set centre without overcooking the outside.

Allow to cool, then refrigerate before decorating with whipped cream and ginger pieces.

serves 6 - 8

preparation time 30 minutes

ingredients

Base:

- 75g butter
- 125g ginger nut biscuits, finely crushed

Filling:

- 300g pumpkin, peeled and de-seeded
- 1 $\frac{1}{2}$ tblspns ginger in syrup, finely chopped
- 375g low or medium fat soft cheese, softened
- 75g caster sugar
- finely grated rind and juice of 1 lemon
- 2 eggs
- 150ml double or whipping cream, whipped until stiff
- extra ginger pieces, roughly chopped for decoration

baking

The use of dark brown sugar or black treacle in cakes, icings and toppings on sponge cakes, or glazing fruit cakes with melted honey or apricot jam all help to darken the appearance of microwave baked cakes. True, when cooked, they are lighter in colour when compared to cakes baked conventionally. However, microwave cakes have a really fresh moist flavour and texture that makes up for any lack of colour - not to mention that they are cooked in a fraction of the time taken conventionally so saving on energy costs.

Have a look at the two versions of the Celebration Cake on page 72. The paler coloured cake in the large picture was made with Demerara sugar, whilst the darker one in the small picture – that looks as though it was baked in a conventional oven, was made with dark soft brown sugar. You can see just how much difference these subtle differences make, but both look great and appetizing to eat.

For the best results always cook cakes and puddings on an elevated rack. This helps the microwaves to penetrate from the bottom and sides as well as the top and gives a much better and more even cook throughout the cake.

Packet cake mixes cook particularly well in the microwave oven (see the recipe for Quick Black forest upside down pudding on page 80), As a general rule, substitute half the added liquid required for oil; this helps keep the cake moist both during and after cooking.

Also, add one extra tablespoon of water to the total mixture. Today's high powered ovens cook cakes quickly and evenly in minutes. If the cake mixture is divided into 2 x 18 - 20cm cooking containers, cook both on the same shelf of the oven on MEDIUM HIGH for 3 - 4 minutes until well-risen and set. If the cake mixture is cooked in 1 x 18 - 20 cm round dish, it will take 7 - 8 minutes to cook on MEDIUM HIGH.

Remember to leave the cake in the cooking container for 5 - 10 minutes standing time after cooking, before turning out.

But don't forget the microwave oven has other great uses to help with baking - like proving bread dough. Most people don't bake bread at home any more because of the long time delay in waiting for the dough to 'prove'

then 'rise'. Doughs 'prove' quite successfully in the microwave oven; useful especially in cold weather, when it can be difficult to find an area in the home warm enough to do the job adequately.

To prove: place the prepared dough in a floured bowl. HEAT on MEDIUM LOW for 1 minute, then rest for 5 minutes. Repeat this process twice. By this time the dough will have doubled in size. Continue following the recipe instructions, then place the dough in a greased baking tin. Allow the dough to 'rise' again, using the same process as above, but once the bread has reached the top of the tin do not microwave any more. Allow it to complete its rising, unaided, covered with a warm damp cloth, otherwise the microwaves could start to cook the loaf.

During baking, too much microwave energy creates large air pockets in the dough by cooking it too quickly, and gives an unsatisfactory appearance. For the best results the bread should go into a pre-heated oven. On completion the bread should sound hollow when tapped on the base.

traditional steamed sponge pudding

I've chosen to make a Syrup pudding here, but as this recipe is so versatile there really is no end to the varieties of pudding you can make with this basic recipe - omit the golden syrup and 25g of the flour, but add 25g cocoa powder, an extra 25g sugar and the finely grated rind and juice of 1 orange to the basic sponge mixture to make a chocolate orange pudding, or add 2 teaspoons instant coffee and 50g roughly chopped walnuts to make a coffee and walnut pudding; or even the finely grated rind and juice of 2 lemons, plus an extra 25g sugar to make a lemon sponge - all cook in the same way and are delicious. Look at how long they take to cook as well - minutes instead of hours!

Cream the softened butter and sugar together in a mixing bowl until light and fluffy. Add the eggs, milk and sieved flour. Beat mixture until it forms a stiff smooth batter.

Grease thoroughly a 1 - 1.5 litre oven-proof pudding basin, jug or bowl. Carefully spoon golden syrup into base, then pour in cake batter.

Cover top of bowl with a sheet of greaseproof paper. Cook on MEDIUM HIGH for 8 - 9 minutes, until well-risen and spongy to touch and cooked through. Leave to stand for 2 - 3 minutes before turning out to serve.

Serve with custard or ice cream.

serves 4 - 6
preparation time 10 minutes

ingredients

- 175g butter, softened
- 125g caster sugar
- 3 eggs, beaten
- 100ml milk
- 175g self raising flour, sieved
- 2 - 3 tblspns golden syrup - or to taste

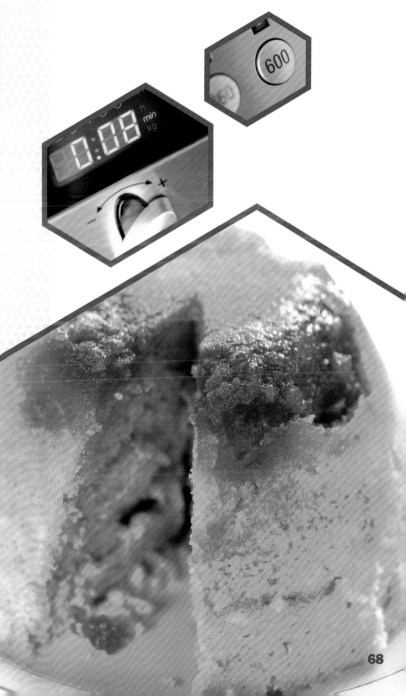

the 2 ½ minute family sponge

home made sponge:

If you haven't built up the confidence to make a home made sponge yet – cheat and use a packet cake mix. Using this method, both will give great results. Bake the two separate halves of the cake one at a time in an 18cm ovenproof cake dish. You will get a finished cake that is almost 10cm high and that's without any filling! So, amaze yourself and give this one a try!

Place all ingredients into a large mixing bowl. Using an electric beater on low speed, beat for 1 minute, then increase speed and beat for 3 - 4 minutes until mixture is smooth, light and creamy.

Divide cake mixture between 2 well greased 18cm cake pans. Bake each cake separately on MEDIUM HIGH for 2 ½ minutes. The cake may be a little sticky to touch on the surface, but a skewer or sharp knife inserted into the centre of the cake should come out clean. Allow to stand, covered for 5 minutes. Turn out on to a wire rack to cool.

Serve sandwiched together with jam and whipped cream and the top dusted with sieved icing sugar.

packet cake mix:

Make up the cake mix, according to instructions on the packet, use the 2 eggs and additional oil and water, and add at the beginning of the beating stage. The extra egg helps beat more air into the mixture, while the addition of a little more oil helps keep the cake moist and fresh for longer.

Combine ingredients using an electric beater, beat on low speed for 1 minute, then increase speed and beat for 3 - 4 minutes until mixture is smooth, light and creamy.

Pour half of cake mixture into the well greased 18cm cake pan. Bake on MEDIUM HIGH for 2 ½ minutes. Cake may be a little sticky to touch on the top, but a skewer or sharp knife inserted into the centre of the cake should come out clean. The surface will dry out on standing. After cooking, the cake should come away from the sides of the cooking dish easily. Allow to stand for 5 minutes, before turning out on to a wire rack to cool.

Re-grease cooking container and cook remaining half of cake mixture in the same way.

preparation time 6 - 8 minutes

ingredients

home made sponge:

- 175g self raising flour, sieved
- 175g sugar
- 175g butter, softened
- 3 eggs
- 100ml milk
- 1 teaspn vanilla extract

preparation time 6 - 7 minutes

packet cake mix:

- 220g packet of cake mix
- 2 eggs
- 6 tblspns cooking oil
- 2 tblspns water

sticky black gingerbread

Line a 23cm square oven-proof cake dish with greaseproof paper.

Sieve flour, bicarbonate of soda and spices together into a bowl.Place the butter, brown sugar, syrup and treacle into a 1 litre oven-proof bowl. Heat on HIGH for 1 minute until butter is melted.

Beat the milk and eggs together, then stir into sugar mixture. Lastly, stir in flour and spices.

Pour mixture into prepared cake pan and cook on MEDIUM HIGH for 6 - 7 minutes, until spongy to touch and when a sharp knife is inserted into the centre of the cake, it comes out clean. Cover dish with a dinner plate and leave to stand for 10 minutes.

Leave to cool completely before cutting into squares.

ingredients

- 350g plain flour
- 2 teaspns bicarbonate of soda
- 2 teaspns ground ginger
- 2 teaspns ground cinnamon
- 250g butter
- 250g soft dark brown sugar
- 125g golden syrup
- 125g black treacle
- 225ml milk
- 2 eggs, beaten

peanut butter and jam muffins

I couldn't decide whether to put this recipe into the 'Cooking, Carb's and Kids' chapter or this one, as really it's a great recipe for kids to make, but also shows how versatile the microwave oven is for quick baking.
Perfect for lunch boxes or with a glass of milk after school, these muffins are also great to use up left over jam of any flavour.

Mix together the flour, porridge oats, and sugar in a mixing bowl. Put the peanut butter into a separate large bowl, soften in the microwave oven on HIGH for 30 seconds. Add the oil, egg and milk and beat together until smooth.

Stir in the flour mixture until well blended.

Place 1 teaspoon of the mixture into 6 muffin cases in an individual cake pan or set in a circle on the glass turntable. Put a teaspoon of jam on top of each muffin, then cover with another teaspoon of muffin mixture. Sprinkle tops with chopped nuts.

Cook on HIGH for 2 minutes until well risen, spongy to touch and when a knife inserted into the centre of each comes out clean.

Repeat process until all mixture has been used. Leave to cool on a wire rack.

makes 12 - 14 muffins
preparation time 15 minutes

ingredients

- 125g self raising flour
- 75g porridge oats
- 50g dark soft brown sugar
- 75g peanut butter - smooth or crunchy works equally well
- 1 tblspn cooking oil
- 1 egg
- 200ml milk
- 2 - 3 tblspns strawberry or raspberry jam
- 50g roast peanuts, roughly chopped

celebration ring

Cooked in minutes, this delicious cake is a good example of how well rich fruit and nut cakes cook in the microwave oven in a fraction of the time traditionally taken. This is one of my favourites, great for Christmas, glazed with honey instead of icing; it keeps perfectly in a sealed tin for up to a month.

Grease a 20 cm round cake ring and place a ring of greased parchment paper in the base.

Place the nuts and fruit into a large mixing bowl.

Sieve the flour, mixed spices and baking powder on top with the sugar.

Lightly beat the eggs and brandy or fruit juice together and stir into the fruit and nut mixture until well combined. Spoon mixture into cake ring.

Bake on MEDIUM HIGH for 10 - 12 minutes. Test if cake is cooked in the centre with a wooden skewer. When cooked, leave in the container to stand for 10 minutes before turning out onto a wire rack to cool.

Warm honey on HIGH for 30 seconds and use to glaze cake.

ingredients

- 125g brazil nuts, left whole
- 125g broken walnuts
- 125g almonds
- 50g dates, stoned and halved
- 125g raisins
- 225g red and green glace cherries
- 125g mixed dried fruit
- 150g plain flour, sieved
- 1 teaspn mixed spice
- $1/_2$ teaspn baking powder
- 75g Demerara sugar
- 3 eggs, lightly beaten
- 2 tblspns brandy or fruit juice
- 2 tblspns honey

have you thought about... jams and preserves?

I make no apologies for including a chapter on what may be seen as old fashioned in this book about 21st century cooking. Why? Because jams and preserves cooked in the microwave oven are bright, colourful and as full of flavour as when the fruit was picked. What is more, they are free from any additives and need no preservatives.

Tasting is believing.

The recipe for Whisky marmalade is the best I have ever tasted, and the strawberry jam delicious. So see for yourself!

The cooking method is also clean, there are no large preserving pans to watch and prevent from burning. It's quick, 1 - 2 kilos of jam, chutney or pickle can be made in under an hour. It's safe - the boiling sugar syrup is cooked behind a locked door, away from inquisitive fingers.

Lastly, it's economical; small amounts of jam can be made that are ideal to give away as inexpensive gifts.

here are some tips to help:

to sterilize the jars:

Pour approximately 2 - 3 cms of boiled water into each thoroughly washed and dried jar. Place in the microwave oven and heat, on HIGH until the water boils. Remove jars as they are ready - but use oven gloves, they will be hot! Place caps on jars quickly and leave while making jam, but do not forget to empty out the water before filling with prepared jam.

Choose a large cooking vessel that is suitable for the job. Jam contains a lot of moisture and sugar, so it is likely to boil up over four times its own volume during cooking. Ensure the fruit and sugar mixture only fills one quarter of the cooking container prior to cooking.

The chosen container must also be able to withstand high temperatures, so choose it carefully. If choosing plastic, look on the packaging or the base of the container; the manufacturer will recommend a cooking temperature the container can withstand. Pyrex or oven-proof glass is ideal. Try to use one that has straight sides, not sloping ones.

to check the setting point:

Dribble a little of the cooked jam on to a cold saucer and leave it in the refrigerator for 2 minutes. If a skin forms on top, which wrinkles when pushed with a finger, setting point is reached. Alternatively, dip a spoon into the syrup and raise it above the bowl.

A single drop should remain suspended from the spoon for a few seconds. However, the most accurate and safest method is to use a cooking thermometer. Jams will set when they reach a temperature of 106°C.

Pickles and chutneys improve with age. So, if possible, store for at least a month before consuming. Jam, if poured into sterilized jars and sealed properly, will keep for up to one year.

Lastly wash and choose the fruit carefully before using. Discard any bruised or over-ripe pieces. You cannot make good quality jam from poor quality ingredients.

whisky marmalade

If you can find a better tasting marmalade, I'll be amazed. Use small jars and fill 6 instead of 3 or 4 larger ones to give away as presents.

Coarsely grate the rind and squeeze the juice from all the fruit. Cut the orange and lemon skins into pieces and place in a muslin bag with the fruit pips*. Tie securely and place this bag into cooking container with juice and rind. Stir in the boiling water. Cook on HIGH for 20 minutes, stirring frequently throughout cooking.

Stir juice mixture well, squeeze the muslin bag** tightly to release the concentrated juices and remove from liquid. Stir in the whisky, sugars and black treacle. Continue cooking on HIGH for a further 50 - 60 minutes, stirring occasionally, until jam reaches setting point or 106°C when tested with a thermometer.

Stir well and pour into sterilized jars. Seal quickly and label.

*Note: if no muslin or large square of cotton are to hand, use one of the little bags that accompany washing powder tablets. A new clean one works a treat!
**As the muslin bag will be very hot, wear rubber gloves or place the bag in a sieve and squeeze with a wooden spoon.

makes 3 x 300g jars
preparation time
30 - 40 minutes

ingredients

- 3 large juicy oranges
- 1 large lemon
- 250ml boiling water
- 150ml whisky
- 350g white sugar
- 350g soft brown sugar
- 2 tblspns black treacle

strawberry jam

This is a great basic recipe. Any variation of fruit can be substituted for strawberries, but the cooking times will vary slightly; raspberries taking slightly less time to cook and loganberries, a mixture of apples and blackberries, or blueberries taking longer to cook before they tenderize. The recipe is the same. Use equal quantities of fruit and sugar, and add lemon juice to help the setting properties, as these fruit contain little pectin of their own.

Do not add any additional water. Again, as there is no direct heat source, the jam can't burn or stick to the bottom of the pan, but it does need stirring frequently throughout the cooking procedure.

Don't forget too, that the cooking container will be very hot, so wear oven gloves to transfer it from the oven. Set it on a dry surface to avoid both the cooking container and work surface from receiving thermal shock, which could scald the work surface and even crack the cooking dish.

Place the prepared strawberries and lemon rind and juice into a large 2 litre oven-proof dish or casserole. Cover with a well fitting lid or cling wrap and cook on HIGH for 3 minutes. Stir well, then stir in the sugar and continue stirring until all the sugar has dissolved.

Cook on HIGH for a further 20 - 30 minutes, stirring every 5 - 10 minutes until jam reaches its setting point or a temperature of 106°C.

Allow to cool for 3 - 4 minutes before pouring carefully into sterilized jars. Seal and label.

makes: 3 x 250g jars
preparation time 5 minutes

ingredients

- 450g strawberries, washed and hulled
- finely grated rind and juice of 2 large lemons
- 450g white jam sugar

candied fruit

I pondered whether to include another jam or chutney recipe here, but decided on something a little different - a gift - and as time is the greatest gift you can give anyone, this is a great home-made one. Any type of candied fruit is very expensive to buy, and though a little time consuming to make this version is excellent, inexpensive and stores well. It is delicious when used chopped in fruit cakes, mixed with breakfast cereals, or even, as a topping for cakes and crumbles. So, put some in pretty lined boxes, keep some and give some away.

Remove the peel from the fruit, taking care to keep it in neat quarters if possible. Wash thoroughly and remove any white pith that may be still attached. Put peel into an oven-proof bowl. Cover with a well fitting lid or cling wrap and cook on HIGH for 2 minutes, stir well, recover dish and continue cooking on HIGH for 5 minutes until peel is tender.

Stir in the sugar; it will completely dissolve during the cooking process. Continue to cook on MEDIUM HIGH for 5 minutes until the sugar boils together with the peel. Leave to cool then stand in a cool place for 24 hours.

Cook peel in the syrup again on HIGH uncovered for 3 minutes until it boils, then reduce power to MEDIUM and cook for a further 3 minutes. Be careful not to allow the syrup to burn.

Spread on a wire rack and leave to dry out for 24 hours until the remaining sugar coating dries out. Store in an airtight container.

makes: approximately 400g

preparation time
30 - 40 minutes excluding standing times

ingredients

- peel from 4 large oranges, lemons, limes and or mandarins
- 125g caster sugar

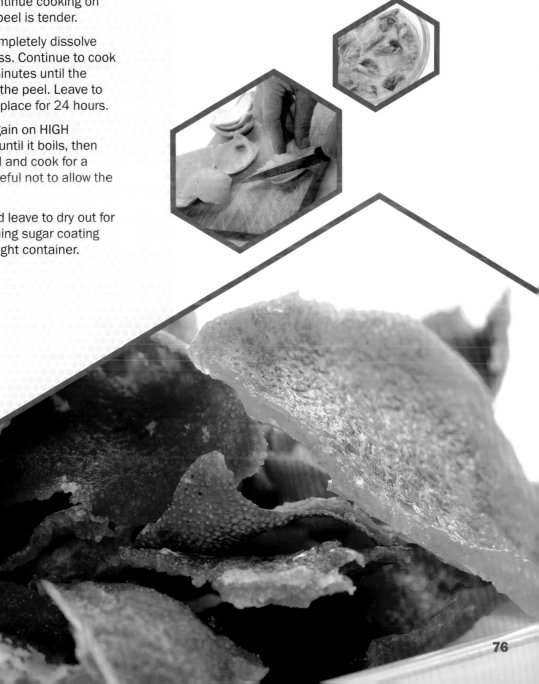

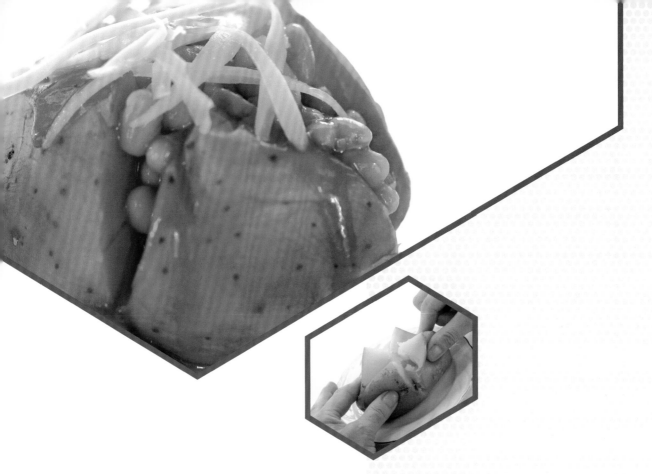

Cooking, Carb's and Kids...

Kids understand microwave ovens, just as they do computers. For some reason, they just automatically know how to use them. Maybe that's because they are not intimidated by them. They may not understand their inner workings, but quite rightly have a confidence for cooking with microwaves - and it shows.

It was said recently that the current generation of children growing up may die before their parents, due to their poor lifestyle and eating habits. Much has been portrayed through the media to encourage families to sit and eat together to create a happy, calm environment, conducive of good eating and, just as important, good digestion and social skills.

Today though, young people relate to fast! Slow is past tense, and that won't change in the near future - just as kitchens and appliances are changing to fit in with 21st century lifestyles. Young people do need to learn how to cook, maybe at the same time as their parents!

The recipes that follow are confidence builders. Some use convenience and pre-weighed packet ingredients, some fresh; but all are great learning tools to assist the cook in getting to know and understand the workings of a microwave oven, before moving on to more complicated recipes.

So get them in the kitchen - hands washed, ready for action!

Let's start with our old favourite:

stuffed baked potatoes

Remember one medium sized potato, cooked in its jacket will take approximately 4 minutes to cook on HIGH; two potatoes will take 5 - 6 minutes. Experiment to find the time that best suits your own oven and use that as your future bench mark.

Potatoes are great natural carbohydrates; the fresher they are the more vitamin C they contain, and are easy for kids and teenagers to cook themselves.

Firstly wash potato(es) well. Prick all over with a fork, so that the skin does not burst during cooking. Set one potato in the centre of the oven; place two potatoes side by side, three in a triangle; four in a square and five or six in a circle around edge of the turntable.

Cook one potato for 4 minutes. Pierce with a sharp knife or gently squeeze with fingers to test if potato is cooked. It should offer a little resistance. Remove from the oven, wrap in foil and leave to stand for 3 - 4 minutes while filling is being prepared.

Cut a cross in the potato, open out a little to expose centre and fill with butter or a topping of your choice; these could include: Baked beans and grated cheese, coleslaw, a mixture of grated cheese and chopped ham or cooked chicken, cooked chilli, Coronation chicken, cooked, flaked smoked fish, tuna or canned salmon, sour cream and chives... the list is endless.

crunchy savoury rice

A great dish for young people to make themselves and eat with friends. Serve with grilled or barbequed chops or sausages. I've also used cups as an additional measurement here to make life easier if no scales are to hand; but use the same sized 'cup' for all the ingredients to ensure perfect results. It's also excellent served cold as a rice salad.

Pour 1.125 litres (3 ½ cups) boiling water into a large 3 litre ovenproof dish or casserole. Stir in the washed rice and stock cube. Cook on HIGH for 10 minutes, stirring well half way through cooking time. Reduce power to MEDIUM and continue cooking for 5 minutes until rice is tender and all liquid has been absorbed. Stir well, cover and leave to stand.

While rice is cooking, prepare vegetables. Place butter, onion and celery into a 2 litre oven-proof dish. Cover with a well fitting lid or cling wrap and cook on HIGH for 2 - 3 minutes, stirring well half-way through cooking time. Stir in the corn, soup, sultanas, peanuts, seasoning to taste, mayonnaise and finally the rice.

Transfer to a large shallow ovenproof dish. Sprinkle with breadcrumbs and parsley. Heat through on MEDIUM for 5 minutes. For a little extra colour, brown the top under a hot grill for 2 - 3 minutes.

serves 6

preparation time 15 minutes

ingredients

- 350g (2 cups) long grain rice, well washed
- 1 chicken stock cube
- 25g butter
- 1 onion, finely chopped
- 2 sticks celery, finely sliced
- 250ml can sweetcorn kernels, drained
- 240g can condensed cream of chicken soup
- 50g (½ cup) sultanas
- 100g (1 cup) peanuts
- black pepper to taste
- 3 tblspns mayonnaise
- 3 tblspns breadcrumbs
- 2 tblspns fresh chopped parsley

cheese and pepperoni chicken

Substitute any variety of cheese or ham for the Gouda and Pepperoni in this recipe. With chicken breasts or thighs usually to be found in most freezers, it's also a great store cupboard recipe that the older kids can make for themselves. Serve it with pasta or rice and a tomato based sauce.

Place a piece of greaseproof paper on the work surface, lay chicken on paper and cover with another piece of paper. Flatten chicken with a rolling pin until 1 cm thick all over.

Cover each piece of chicken with a sprinkle of cheese, then Pepperoni. Roll up chicken and secure with a cocktail stick.

Place in a shallow oven-proof dish or plate. Cover with a well fitting lid or cling wrap and cook on MEDIUM HIGH for 5 - 6 minutes until cooked through. Meat will be white throughout and juices will run clear when pierced with a sharp knife.

Leave to stand for 3 - 4 minutes before serving.

serves 4
preparation time 10 minutes

ingredients

- 4 boned chicken breasts or large boned thighs
- 125g Gouda cheese, grated
- 50g Pepperoni sliced

black forest upside down pudding

This has always been a great favourite of my children - not to mention the fact that this recipe just can't fail!
You can even watch it rise in the oven as it cooks.

Pour the contents of the packet of chocolate cake mix into a greased 2 litre ovenproof dish or casserole. Add the eggs, cooking oil and water. Beat together until smooth; scrape down mixture from sides of dish.

Open a can of black cherry pie filling, pour over cake mixture. Cook on MEDIUM HIGH for 7 - 8 minutes; until the cake mixture has risen through the pie filling, is well risen and should feel spongy to touch. Cover with a dinner plate and leave to stand for 1 - 2 minutes.

Serve pudding straight from the dish or place a large dinner plate on top of dish. Quickly turn dish upside down so that the pudding falls on to the plate.

Serve immediately with chocolate sauce and/or ice cream.

serves 4

preparation time 6 - 8 minutes

ingredients

- 220g packet of chocolate cake mixture
- 2 large eggs
- 6 tblspns cooking oil
- 2 tblspns water
- 385g can black cherry pie filling

ingredients

- 75g butter
- 75g Demerara sugar
- 1 tblspn cocoa powder
- $1/2$ teaspn vanilla essence
- 25g mixed peel, chopped or dried apricots, chopped
- 200g brown bread crumbs

icing:

- 25g butter
- 50g icing sugar, sieved
- 1 tblspn cocoa powder, dissolved in
- 1 - 2 tblspns boiling water
- 25g butter

chocolate fudge fingers

Made with left over brown bread crumbs, these are rich, sweet and delicious. Good for lunch box snacks that don't cost the earth!

Put the butter, sugar and cocoa powder into a medium-sized oven-proof bowl. Heat on HIGH for 2 minutes until butter melts and sugar dissolves; stir well after 1 minute. Stir in remaining ingredients, mix well then press into a 21cm well greased loose-bottomed cake dish. Refrigerate until set.

icing: soften butter on HIGH for 15 seconds, beat in remaining ingredients, adding a little more boiling water if necessary to form a stiff icing. Spread over biscuit base.

When icing sets, ease out of cake dish and cut into fingers to serve.

pear, peach and pineapple crisp

This is a variation on the good old fashioned 'crumble', so use any variety or combination of fruit to suit the time of year. Canned or frozen fruit is great in winter; fresh peaches, nectarines and plums are delicious in summer.

Place prepared pears, peach slices and pineapple pieces in a large 2 - 3 litre ovenproof dish or casserole. Sprinkle with lemon juice. Cover with a well-fitting lid or cling wrap and cook on HIGH for 3 - 4 minutes until almost soft (al-dente). Set dish side.

Combine remaining ingredients in a large oven-proof bowl. Cook on HIGH for 2 - 3 minutes until hot and butter has melted. Stir well half way through cooking time.

Spread the mixture over fruit. Cook on MEDIUM HIGH for 8 - 10 minutes until fruit is soft and topping crisps up.

Serve hot or cold with whipped cream.

serves 4 - 6

preparation time 10 minutes

ingredients

- 4 pears, peeled, cored and roughly sliced
- 1 fresh peach, washed and sliced
- 3 pineapple rings, chopped
- 3 tblspns lemon juice
- 125g brown sugar
- 125g quick cook porridge oats
- 50g plain flour
- 75g butter, cut into 1 cm chunks
- 2 teaspns cinnamon
- $\frac{1}{2}$ teaspn ground nutmeg

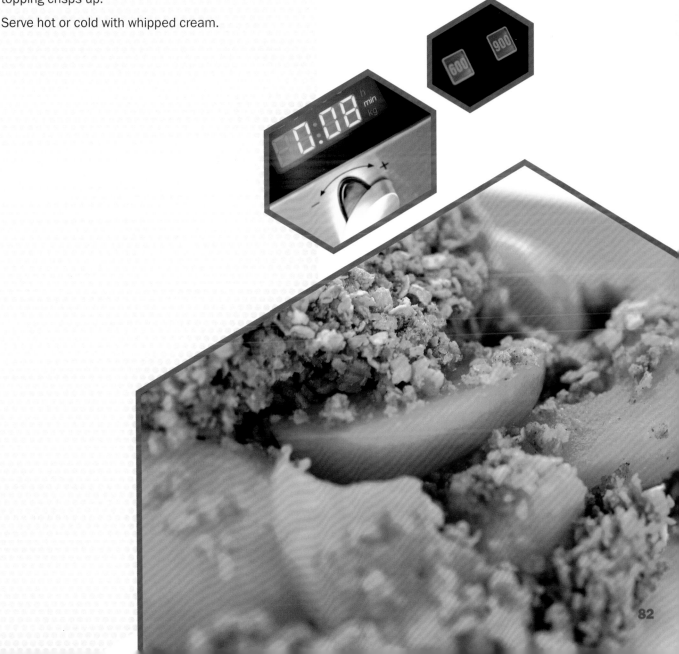

great food for toddlers - getting a head start

Now there are no excuses! Research has shown that eating habits are often laid down for life, starting with the first solids given to toddlers. My own children ate these dishes as toddlers and under 5's. The results - obviously, they are fit and healthy, but as vegetables formed a major part of their basic diet when young, they never developed a taste for either salt, sugar or quick snack foods. Today, as adults, they have a choice as to what they eat; however they find the flavour of most crisps, biscuits etc., quite unpalatable, so they choose not to eat food that contains any unnecessary additives.

Cooking toddlers' meals in a microwave oven takes no longer then opening a can. A week's supply of toddler food can be prepared in less than 20 minutes. The difference too is that the meals are fresh, nourishing, home made and cost a fraction of the bought product.

Why not make up batches of these recipes and freeze them in small quantities - enough for each meal in ice cube trays and store them in the freezer. 1 or 2 cubes are ideal for 6 - 9 month old babies, 3 or 4 cubes are ideal for toddlers.

Thaw the cubes in the microwave oven, stir well, then reheat gently for a great instant meal. Don't forget to test for temperature yourself before feeding them to a child. Cook these recipes in small quantities at first then double or treble the recipe for extra children or for batch freezing.

plain mashed potato

Peel and chop 1 medium sized potato into small 1 - 2 cm cubes. Rinse and place into a small cooking dish. Cover with a well fitting lid and cook on HIGH for 4 - 5 minutes.

Add 15gms (1 teaspoon) butter and 2 tablespoons milk. Mash until smooth and creamy.

Use this as a basis for other vegetable dishes, a topping for meat or fish dishes, or as a vegetable by itself.

Use immediately, or spoon into ice cube trays and freeze for future use.

mixed vegetable medley

Peel and chop 1 small potato into small 1 - 2 cm cubes; do the same with 75gms of pumpkin or squash, and 1 carrot. Rinse and place into a small cooking dish. Cover with a well fitting lid and cook on HIGH for 4 - 5 minutes. If desired add 1 tablespoon frozen peas. Return to the oven, cook for a further 1 - 1 $^1/_2$ minutes, add 15 gms (1 teaspoon) butter and 2 - 3 tablespoons milk. Mash until smooth and creamy.

Use some immediately and freeze the remainder in ice cube trays for use later. Once frozen, the cubes may be released from the ice-cube trays and stored in a polythene bag, this keeps the trays free for other uses. This recipe is lovely. 1 - 2 ice cubes-full make a great little lunch or dinner for a toddler; it's bright, colourful and packed with vegetable goodness. 3 - 4 cubes added to some cooked pasta makes a great meal for a pre-school child. Have you noticed how little waste there is, and how little washing up?

bubble and squeak

Stir 1 beaten egg and 1 tablespoon finely chopped and cooked savoy cabbage into 1 plain mashed potato recipe. Cook on HIGH for 1 $^1/_2$ - 2 minutes until the egg is just beginning to set. Stir well and if necessary stir in a couple of teaspoons of milk to soften and cool it down before eating. Great for 12 - 18 month old toddlers. Freeze the remainder in ice cube trays. Defrost slowly.

beef and cheese pasta

In a small casserole dish mix together 3 tablespoons of cottage cheese, a chopped tomato, 2 tablespoons of fresh minced beef, 2 tablespoons of small uncooked pasta shells or small twists and 3 tablespoons of water. Cover dish and cook on MEDIUM HIGH for 8 - 10 minutes, stirring occasionally during cooking until all water has been absorbed and pasta and meat are almost cooked through. After 1 - 2 minutes standing time, you will find that the pasta and meat complete

their cooking and absorb any excess moisture in the dish. This makes 2 good sized meals and is great for 18 - 24 month old toddlers.

spanish omelette

Put 1 - 2 tablespoons of any left over cooked vegetables (e.g. peas, carrots, potatoes, tomato, broccoli, baked beans or even some of the mixed vegetable medley) puréed, mashed or left whole (according to feeding stage) in a small oven-proof dish. Pour 1 beaten egg over the vegetables. Cook on MEDIUM for 1 minute, stir well, then continue cooking on MEDIUM for a further 1 - 1 $^1/_2$ minutes until egg just begins to set. Cover dish and leave to stand for 1 - 2 minutes to allow the egg to complete its cooking without turning it into rubber. Vegetables should also be warmed through. Serve Immediately.

fruit bread sticks

This is a great way to use up left over malt loaf, fruit bread, pancetta or even wholemeal bread. The sticks are suitable for any age to suck and chew.

Cut the slices of bread into large fingers. Place on a piece of kitchen paper on the glass plate of the microwave oven. Cook for 5 - 6 minutes on HIGH, until the bread has dried out completely, removing the ones at the outer edges as they cook. Store in an airtight tin.

heating baby foods and milk

Contrary to what you might have ever read in the past, heating baby food and milk in the microwave oven is both safe and efficient and does not diminish any of the nutrients in the food.

However like any other heating method the food or milk must be stirred or shaken, then tested for an acceptable temperature before being fed to any baby or child. Heat a 125ml bottle of baby milk for no longer than 45 seconds on MEDIUM power to warm it through thoroughly, or a 225ml bottle for 60 seconds on MEDIUM. Remember to test the temperature before giving it to a baby or toddler to drink.

playing dough

This last recipe isn't for eating - though I get asked for it a lot - and have purposely measured out the ingredients in cups as well as in grams. At the playgroup, nursery or when just wanting to get the children involved, weighing scales are not always to hand. This way, as long as the same cup is used for all the measuring, the end result will work out perfectly.

Use different shades of food colouring and make up 4 - 6 separate doughs - great for inspiration and boundless imagination.

Add a little of the food colour to the water. Set aside.

Place the flour, cream of tartar and salt into a large mixing bowl, stir to mix ingredients thoroughly together. Make a well in the centre of the flour, pour in the oil and coloured water. Using your hand, mix all ingredients together to form a stiff dough.

Add a little extra flour if necessary to form a stiff and workable dough, but not too much, as it solidifies on cooking. Place ball of dough on an oven-proof plate; flatten slightly so that it is a circle of about 2 - 3cm thick. Cook on MEDIUM for 5 - 6 minutes. Quickly knead dough into a pliable ball. If it's too hot to touch, wear rubber gloves. Allow dough to cool thoroughly before using.

Store in an airtight container in the refrigerator when not in use.

To make dough pliable again, heat through on MEDIUM LOW for 30 seconds.

ingredients

- few drops of food colour
- $^3/_4$ cup (200ml) water
- 1 cup (150g) plain flour
- 1 tblspn cream of tartar
- $^1/_4$ cup (25g) salt
- 1 tblspn cooking oil

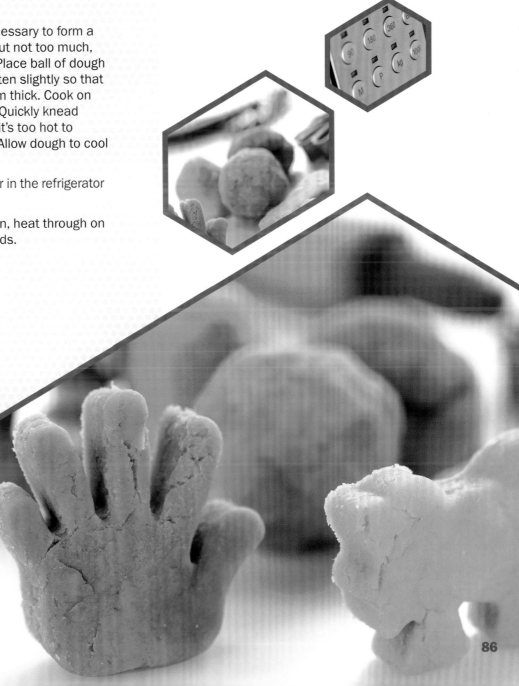

only got 20 minutes?

No time to cook dinner or prepare a meal for unexpected guests... nonsense! Use a can or open a packet to prepare a dinner that is wholesome and home cooked in under 20 minutes.

With the advent of advanced food production systems, all canned food produced nowadays is processed literally within hours of being picked. The food is therefore fresh and must be of first class quality, otherwise the colour, shape, texture and flavour of the finished product would be unacceptable to anyone opening the can.

Nutrients too are retained. The canning procedure involves only 'blanching' or lightly cooking, so most of the nutrients in the fresh produce are retained. The vitamin part of your meal can be supplied with fresh cooked vegetables.

On opening the can you will see all the peeling, chopping, dicing and slicing has been done for you. So, using your microwave oven, store cupboard ingredients and a little imagination, feeding the family when you are feeling tired and hungry need not be a problem.

Cans and packets are not only good stand-bys for emergency meals, they can also add a lift to any quickly prepared meal. For example, heat a 275g can of condensed cream of mushroom soup as a sauce for grilled lamb chops or chicken.

Use a can of condensed French onion soup as a sauce to serve with grilled steak, beef olives; or a packet of flavoured stuffing mix instead of plain breadcrumbs in savoury recipes or toppings.

All the recipes in this chapter form part of complete meals, so the washing up is kept to a minimum as well.

But, don't forget - never place an unopened can or opened can of food into the oven to heat by ANY cooking method. Always pour the contents into an oven-proof container and heat, covered with a well-fitting lid or cling wrap. This keeps the food moist, minimises cooking times, prevents spattering and reduces loss of flavour. Also don't store opened part-used cans of food in the fridge. Decant into a suitable sealable container to store correctly.

apricot chicken

This dish could not be easier to make, yet the flavour and colour are excellent. Try serving it with lemon couscous or French beans and rice. To save on washing up, this dish also cooks well in a 'cook-bag'.

Blend apricots and juice together with the soup mix in a blender or food processor until smooth. Place chicken pieces in a large shallow oven-proof dish or cook bag, pour over the apricot mixture.

Cover with a well fitting lid, cling wrap or seal cook bag. Cook on HIGH for 3 minutes. Re-arrange chicken in dish or bag and continue cooking on MEDIUM for 12 - 15 minutes until chicken is thoroughly cooked. Leave to stand while vegetables are being cooked.

serves 4

preparation time 5 minutes

ingredients

- 411g can apricots in natural juice
- 40g packet dry French onion soup mix
- 4 skinned and boned chicken breasts or 8 thighs, cut into equal sized chunks

pork spare ribs with barbeque sauce

Lovely in the winter served with rice, to mop up all the lovely sauce, or cook in the microwave oven for the first 15 minutes, then finish off on the barbeque in summer. That way, you can ensure the centre is thoroughly cooked and so safe to eat, in a fraction of the time it would usually take.

serves 4

preparation time 5 minutes

ingredients

- 1 onion , roughly chopped
- 2 tblspns honey
- 2 tblspns soy sauce
- 2 tblspns Worcestershire sauce
- 3 tblspns redcurrent jelly
- 2 tblspns lemon juice
- 1 heaped teaspn prepared mustard
- $1/2$ teaspn ground ginger
- 100ml apple juice
- 12 or 16 pork spare rib chops, according to size and appetite
- 1 teaspn cornflour

Place all the ingredients for the marinade in a large cook bag, seal top and set on a oven-proof plate. Heat on HIGH for 1 minute, open bag stir well, and add the spare ribs. Move ribs around in bag to ensure all are coated with marinade. Re-seal bag and set in a shallow oven-proof dish. If time permits leave in refrigerator overnight for ribs to absorb all the flavours.

Cook on HIGH for 5 minutes, re-arrange ribs in sauce again, re-seal bag and continue cooking on MEDIUM HIGH for 15 minutes, stirring and turning ribs after 10 minutes. Ribs should be well cooked. Remove from bag and set on a warm serving plate. Stir cornflour with 1 tablespoon cold water in a small bowl, then stir into marinade ingredients, re-seal bag again and continue cooking on HIGH for 1 - 2 minutes, until marinade boils and thickens. Stir sauce again, then, just before serving, pour over ribs. Serve immediately.

roast duck with sautéd potatoes and onions

serves 2

preparation time 6-7 minutes

ingredients

- 2 large potatoes, peeled and cut into small cubes
- 1 onion, sliced
- 2 tblspns cooking oil
- 25g butter
- 2 large duck breasts, preferably with skin on
- 2 slices orange

Just under the skin of a duck there is a lot of fat, that helps it cook perfectly in a microwave oven, but it does need to be drained off as it cooks. So stand the duck breast on an elevated rack inside the cooking dish, that way, the finished meat is moist and full of flavour, but not greasy.

Rinse the potatoes under cold running water, drain and put into a shallow oven-proof dish with the onion slices. Cover with a well fitting lid or cling wrap and cook on HIGH for 5 minutes.

Put the oil and butter into a frying pan and heat on the top of the stove until hot. Add the potatoes and onion slices, toss well, so that they are well coated with the oily butter, lower heat and continue to cook until golden brown and crispy.

Meanwhile cut slits in the skin of the duck breasts. Set them, skin side down on an elevated rack in a shallow oven proof dish. Cover with a well fitting lid or cling wrap and cook on HIGH for 2 minutes, Turn breast skin side up, reduce power, re-cover dish and continue cooking on MEDIUM for 7 - 8 minutes, until duck is thoroughly cooked. Leave to stand for 2 - 3 minutes, while sauted potato and onion mixture is being transferred to a large warm serving plate.

Remove skin from duck, slice breasts thinly. Set on top of potatoes. Finish by garnishing with a slice of orange.

satay sausages with mashed potatoes

Cook potatoes and satay sauce for this dish in the microwave oven while the sausages cook under a hot grill, for extra speed. Serve with broccoli, peas and sliced carrots.

Prick sausages and place on grill pan. Grill for 10 - 12 minutes turning frequently until thoroughly cooked through.

While sausages are cooking, put prepared potatoes into a large oven-proof dish. Cover with a well fitting lid and cook on HIGH for 8 - 9 minutes, giving dish a good shake or stir half-way through cooking time until potatoes are thoroughly cooked. Stir in butter and milk and mash until smooth.

Place onion in an oven-proof dish, cover and cook on HIGH for 1 minute; stir in the soup, peanut butter and paprika pepper to taste. Heat mixture on HIGH for 3 - 4 minutes stirring occasionally until soup is hot and peanut butter is evenly distributed throughout.

Pile potato on to a warm serving plate, top with sausages, then cover with a little of the sauce. Serve remaining sauce in a sauceboat.

serves 4

preparation time 10 minutes

ingredients

- 8 - 12 large sausages
- 500g potatoes, peeled, washed and cut into small chunks
- 25g butter
- 3 tblspns milk
- 1 large onion, finely chopped
- 400g can tomato soup
- 4 tblspns crunchy peanut butter
- paprika pepper to taste

lamb curry with potato sambals and poppadums

A good curry and poppadums cooked in a microwave in just 20 minutes, whatever next - the surprises just keep coming! Serve with rice, to mop up all the lovely sauce.

Mix the curry powder and cornflour together in a plastic bag or mixing bowl, add the lamb chunks, lemon juice and rind, and leave to marinade for as long as possible - overnight if you can really plan ahead.

Place the onion and ginger into a large oven-proof dish or casserole. Cover with a well fitting lid or cling wrap and cook on HIGH for 1 minute until onion softens. Add reserved pineapple juice, tomatoes and soy sauce. Re-cover dish and cook on HIGH for 4 - 5 minutes until sauce boils. Stir lamb into casserole together with the dates. Re-cover dish and continue cooking on MEDIUM HIGH for 12 - 15 minutes until lamb is tender. Stir in pineapple pieces and continue cooking on MEDIUM HIGH for 2 minutes. Stir well, re-cover dish and leave to stand for 5 minutes. Adjust seasonings to taste.

Meanwhile, toss drained potatoes in the coconut and place in a shallow oven-proof dish. Re-heat on HIGH for 2 minutes until hot.

to cook poppadums: place poppadums well apart on the middle rack in the microwave oven. Cook 4 at a time on HIGH for 1 minute until crisp and puffy.

serves 4

preparation time
10 - 15 minutes

ingredients

- 2 tblspns curry powder
- 2 tblspns cornflour
- 675g neck fillet of lamb, sliced into 2cm chunks
- juice and finely grated rind of 1 lemon
- 1 large onion, chopped
- 1 teaspn fresh root ginger, grated or $1/2$ teaspn powdered ginger
- 450g can pineapple pieces, drained with juice reserved
- 425g can tomatoes
- 2 tblspns soy sauce
- 50g dates
- 440g can new potatoes, drained
- 125g desiccated coconut
- 4 or 8 poppadums

consider cooking for one or two...

Whether young, middle-aged, divorced or widowed, society has more single people to consider now than ever before. Statistics show that the most undernourished people living in the western world are singles. That's why it is important to have a good nutritious meal every day.

Too much fuss - especially as there are so many other things to do besides cook, sit alone to eat, then wash up alone? Well at least the microwave can help with two of those situations.

In comparison with pre-prepared cook-chill meals, these are excellent. Not only because they are freshly prepared and you know what's in them, but also, as they have only taken minutes to

cook from scratch - sometimes no longer than it takes to re-heat a pre-prepared meal, but they cost a fraction of the price of bought meals.

so from breakfast to dinner, give some of these ideas a try:

porridge

Use the same cup measurement, then you won't have to get the scales out! Put $^1/_2$ cup porridge oats into a large ovenproof bowl, stir in $^1/_2$ cup cold milk, then $^1/_2$ cup boiling water. Stand bowl on a large ovenproof plate.

Cover with a well fitting lid, saucer or cling wrap. Cook on HIGH for 2 minutes. Stir well and serve immediately.

luxury scrambled eggs

Break 2 eggs into a small oven-proof bowl. Add seasonings to taste and 2 tblspns milk. Whisk well until frothy, then cook, uncovered on MEDIUM HIGH for 1 minute, whisk again and continue cooking for a further 30 seconds to a minute, until eggs begins to set around the edge. Cover bowl with a saucer and leave to stand while preparing a slice of toast. Butter toast, top with a thin slice of smoked salmon, ham or cheese; cover with scrambled egg and finish with a topping of fresh dill. Delicious - and no saucepan to wash up!

bacon and egg breakfast baps

Want a bacon and egg breakfast with no fat, in just 5 minutes? Then at long last here's the recipe! This serves one, but easily doubles up.

Either put the bacon on an oven-proof plate and cover with 2 pieces of absorbent kitchen paper or place it on a microwave cooking rack, cover with kitchen paper and cook on HIGH for 3 minutes until bacon is thoroughly cooked and all the excess fat has drained off on to the plate or rack. Set aside.

Put approximately 1 tablespn of water into a small oven-proof dish. Break eggs into dish, pierce the yolks.

Cover most of dish with a lid or cling wrap that has been pierced, so that the build up of steam can escape, and cook on MEDIUM HIGH for 1 ½ minutes until yolk is almost set. (Remember it will complete its cooking on standing).

Cut the bread bap in half, set on a plate, and warm through on HIGH for 15 seconds. Place poached egg on one half of the bread, cover with bacon, tomato ketchup and seasonings to taste, top with remaining half of bap. Eat immediately.

ingredients

- 2 - 3 slices bacon
- 2 eggs
- 1 large soft bread bap
- tomato ketchup
- seasonings to taste

apple stuffed trout

Shield the head and tail of the fish with small pieces of foil to avoid over-cooking them. This can be done at the beginning of the cooking time, then removed half way through, or set in place after 1 - 2 minutes of cooking time, and removed before serving.

Any extra stuffing mix can be frozen to use later. To prepare enough for 2, follow directions as for recipe. Cook 2 fish for 3 - 4 minutes.

Place half the butter in an oven-proof dish, add onion, cover with a well fitting lid or cling wrap and cook on HIGH for 1 minute to soften onion. Stir in bread-crumbs, parsley, apple and seasonings to taste.

Use remaining butter to lightly grease the base of a shallow oven-proof dish large enough to hold the fish. Lay prepared fish in dish, fill the cavity with the stuffing mix and secure with wooden cocktail sticks.

Squeeze lemon juice over fish. Cover with a well fitting lid or cling wrap and cook on MEDIUM HIGH for 2 - 3 minutes.

Check that fish is cooked after the minimum cooking time; it should flake easily when split with a knife if cooked thoroughly. Leave to stand for 2 - 3 minutes before serving - this could be while vegetables are being cooked.

Serve hot with green vegetables.

serves 1

preparation time 10 minutes

ingredients

- 15g butter
- 1 small onion, chopped
- 2 tblspns bread crumbs
- 1 tblspn fresh chopped parsley
- 1 small apple, washed and grated
- seasoning to taste
- 1 large trout, gutted, scaled and washed
- 2 tblspns lemon juice

ham and mushroom risotto

I make and serve this in the same dish, so there's no sticky saucepan to wash up. Add 50g roughly cooked chicken, turkey, tuna or salmon for variety. This recipe serves 2 and freezes well, so make up this amount, eat some now and freeze the remainder for a really quick meal later.

Rinse the rice under cold running water to remove the excess starch, place in an oven-proof dish, pour over boiling chicken stock, stir well and cook on HIGH for 10 minutes.

While rice is cooking, chop ham, prepare vegetables and almonds.

Stir rice again, reduce power to MEDIUM and continue cooking for 5 minutes until rice is completely cooked, (though read the pack instructions on the rice as some varieties take longer than 15 minutes to cook and absorb all the stock).

Cover rice dish with a well fitting lid and set aside while cooking vegetables.

Put butter, onion and pepper into an oven-proof dish. Cover with a well fitting lid and cook on HIGH for 2 minutes; stir in mushrooms, ham and almonds, re-cover and continue cooking on MEDIUM HIGH for 3 - 4 minutes; until onion is tender and mushrooms are soft.

Stir vegetable mixture into rice with parsley, seasonings to taste, and fromage frais. Serve hot.

serves 2

preparation time 15 minutes

ingredients

- 100g ($^1/_2$ cup) long grain rice
- 250ml (1 cup) boiling chicken stock (can be made with a stock cube and water)
- 50g ham, roughly chopped
- 25g butter
- l onion, finely chopped
- $^1/_2$ red pepper, deseeded and chopped
- 125g mushrooms, washed and sliced
- 50g blanched almonds, roughly chopped
- 1 tblspn fresh parsley, roughly chopped
- black pepper to taste
- 1 tblspn fromage frais or soured cream

96

what about...
a romantic dinner for two

menu:

Smoked Salmon and
Spinach Roulade
Pork fillet with Mango Chilli sauce
White and Wild rice
Snow peas (Mange tout),
Gingered Carrots
Garlic bread
White Mousseline with
Raspberry coulis

I can promise you, the whole of this meal can be prepared and cooked in a microwave oven, and will definitely help get the work-life balance into perspective. Whether you are a student or well established in life, sometimes it's good to prepare a meal for someone special - only now the excuse, 'I can't cook,' or 'We haven't got a cooker,' goes out of the window. Half prepared in advance, this meal can all be brought together in less than 1 hour to produce a beautiful meal.

shopping

Fresh:
142ml carton sour cream
Butter
4 eggs
Milk
150ml carton double or
whipping cream
125g smoked salmon
Fresh dill
225g fresh spinach
225g snow peas
2 carrots
2 cloves garlic
Fresh parsley
1 small lime
1 large ripe mango
100g fresh or frozen
raspberries
250g pork fillet or loin
1 small crusty French
bread stick

Store Cupboard:
Seasonings
Ground nutmeg
Soft brown sugar
Ground ginger
Chilli sauce
Soy sauce
Chicken stock
Cornflour
Honey
75g white chocolate
Gelatine
Icing sugar
White and wild rice
Baileys Irish liqueur
(optional)

here's how to prepare it:

Jobs to be done in advance:

It is always better to serve a meal late than be flustered, so read the recipes through at least twice, to be sure in which order you are planning to make the meal. Set the table - this can also be done the evening before, every time you look at it throughout the day, it will make you feel good.

Prepare the salmon and spinach roulade. This is better if served well chilled, as it slices easier and looks more attractive. It sets perfectly, well wrapped in the refrigerator and stores well overnight, though it is not freezable.

Prepare the baking tray for roulade. Use a non-stick baking tray or grease and line a 30 x 20 Swiss roll tin with waxed paper. If no Swiss roll tin is available, make a baking tray for the roulade by turning up and folding the four sides of a piece of waxed paper, holding corners firm with a piece of sellotape, so that the finished size is approximately 30 x 20cm, or large enough to sit comfortably on the turntable of your oven. Sit tray on an oven-proof plate. Brush with oil.

Prepare the dessert and sauce. Both can be made the evening before. The mousse sets properly and the sugar dissolves in the sauce.

Slice the pork fillet and make into butterfly steaks. Prepare marinade, add meat, cover and store in the refrigerator until required. This dish also improves with an overnight marinade as the flavours merge together and the lime juice tenderises the meat.

Make garlic bread, wrap in cling wrap.

30 minutes before meal:

Prepare vegetables, place in cooking/serving dishes, cover and set aside.

Cook rice in a saucepan of boiling water on the hob. It can be cooked in the microwave oven, (see cooking rice in the Vegetarian section on page 47)

but if you only have one oven it will be better used for cooking other dishes.

Unwrap roulade, slice into 1 - 2 cm slices and arrange on serving plates.

Turn mousses out of moulds on to serving plates. Stir sauce well, though do not pour any sauce around mousses until just before serving.

Slice mango. Put dinner plates to warm. Cook pork dish. Allow to stand while vegetables are cooked.

to serve:

Warm the garlic bread, wrapped in kitchen paper for 1 minute in the microwave. Place on table.

Serve roulade.

Arrange pork on dinner plates, garnish with mango, prepared sauce, carrots and snow peas. Serve rice in a separate bowl.

Just before serving dessert, pour a little of the coulis around the base of the mousses, decorate with fresh fruit.

smoked salmon and spinach roulade

It's difficult to make this recipe in small amounts, but this stores well for 3 - 4 days in the refrigerator. Any leftovers make a great lunch. Note: if you buy a pack of pre-washed spinach, re-wash it, as you need the fresh water that adheres to it's leaves to cook it in.

Mix sour cream, smoked salmon and dill together. Chill until required.

Place well washed spinach in an oven-proof container, with only the water that adheres to its leaves. Cover tightly with a well fitting lid or cling wrap and cook on HIGH for 3 minutes, giving dish a good shake half way through cooking time. Stand for 1 minute or so, then squeeze and drain off any excess liquid. (Miss out cooking procedure if using frozen, thawed spinach, but heat it though on HIGH for 1 minute and do ensure that all excess moisture has been squeezed out of it. It is essential to do this, to achieve a perfect result.)

Chop spinach finely with the butter, black pepper and nutmeg. Place in a bowl and stir in the egg yolks.

Whisk the egg whites until dry and form soft peaks. Gently fold into spinach mixture. Carefully spoon into prepared cooking tray (see previous page for preparation details). Cook on MEDIUM HIGH for 3 - 4 minutes until top is just set and centre is still a little sticky to touch, but still cooked thoroughly underneath. Sides should be just spongy.

Turn out the roulade onto a piece of waxed or wet greaseproof paper. (Work quickly at this stage so that the roulade is rolled while it is still warm, to prevent it from cracking). Spread the filling onto the roulade and roll up, like a Swiss roll, using the greaseproof paper as a lift and guide. Wet the paper slightly and securely wrap around roulade. Place in refrigerator to set until required.

to serve: cut into 1 - 2 cm slices, set on serving plate garnished with sprigs of fresh dill.

serves 3 - 4
preparation time 30 minutes

ingredients

- 142ml carton soured cream
- 125g smoked salmon, roughly chopped
- 1 tblspn fresh or 1 teaspn dried chopped dill
- 225g fresh or frozen spinach, well washed and trimmed
- 1 teaspn butter
- fresh ground black pepper
- pinch nutmeg
- 2 eggs, separated

pork fillet with mango chilli sauce

Chicken also goes well with mango, so try this dish with 2 chicken breasts for a change - the flavour is exquisite!

Slice the pork into 2 - 3 cm medallions. Cut each medallion almost in half again, without cutting right through. Open out to give a butterfly shape. Place medallions in between sheets of greaseproof paper and flatten with a meat hammer.

Place in a shallow oven-proof dish, add lime juice, chilli, soy sauce, chicken stock and mashed mango. Toss meat well so that it is all covered in the marinade. Cover with cling wrap and leave to marinade for at least 30 minutes or overnight in the refrigerator.

Re-coat meat with marinade and cook on MEDIUM HIGH for 5 minutes, turning meat over half-way through cooking time. Test if meat is cooked; if not, return to oven for a further 1 - 2 minutes. Remove meat from dish, arrange on warmed plates and garnish with reserved mango slices.

Blend cornflour with 2 tablespoons water, stir into meat juices and marinade with the honey. Heat on HIGH for 1 minute, stirring well after 30 seconds, until mixture boils and thickens.

Serve dish with a little sauce drizzled over meat and mango. Finish with reserved chilli slices.

serves 2

preparation time 15 minutes

ingredients

- 250 - 275g piece whole pork fillet or pork loin
- juice 1 small lime (use lemon if necessary)
- 1 - 2 teaspns fresh chilli, de-seeded and finely sliced (reserve a few slices for garnish)
- 1 teaspn soy sauce
- 2 tblspns chicken stock
- 1 large ripe mango, skinned, halved, flesh removed from stone and cut into slices with remaining half mashed
- 1 teaspn cornflour
- 1 teaspn honey

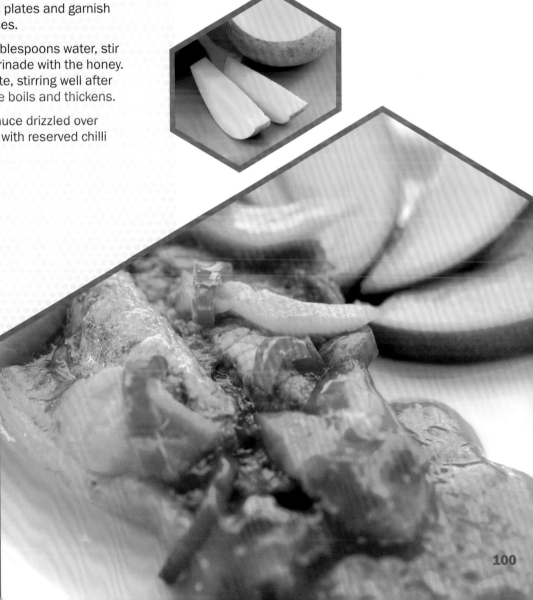

100

white and wild rice

Microwave: follow instructions for cooking rice on page 47 or cook on top of the hob: Wash thoroughly 125g long grain rice and 25g wild rice. Pour 500ml boiling water into a saucepan, stir in the rice, add seasoning to taste. Bring to the boil, reduce heat to a simmer and cook for 15 - 20 minutes until rice is tender. Drain well. Serve immediately.

garlic bread

Cut slits in 1 small crusty French stick without cutting all the way through. Soften 50g butter in the microwave oven on HIGH for 15 seconds, then blend in 2 crushed cloves of garlic and 1 tablespoon of fresh chopped parsley. Spread the flavoured butter into each slice of bread. Wrap whole loaf in kitchen paper and heat through on HIGH for 1 - 2 minutes.

snow peas (mange tout)

Top and tail 225g snow peas, wash and place in a shallow oven-proof dish with 25g butter and a sprinkle of black pepper. Cover dish with a well fitting lid or cling wrap and cook on HIGH for 2 minutes. Give dish a good shake or stir, re-cover and allow to stand for 2 - 3 minutes before serving.

gingered carrots

Melt together 25g butter and 25g soft brown sugar in a medium sized oven-proof dish on HIGH for 1 minute. Stir in $1/2$ teaspoon of ground ginger or 1 tablespoon of finely grated fresh ginger. Stir in 2 washed carrots that have been peeled and cut into thick matchstick lengths. Cover dish with a well fitting lid or cling wrap and cook according to desired crunchiness on HIGH for 2 - 3 minutes.

white mousseline with raspberry coulis

This is heaven for us chocolate lovers. Try coconut liqueur instead of Irish cream liqueur for variety, but don't miss out the raspberry coulis - it finishes off this dish a treat!

Dissolve the chocolate and milk together in a small bowl on MEDIUM for 3 - 4 minutes, stir well until smooth and leave to cool a little. Whip egg whites, and in a separate bowl whisk cream until stiff.

In another small bowl, blend cream liqueur with 1 tablespoon of water and the gelatine. Heat on MEDIUM for 30 seconds, then stir well to ensure gelatine is thoroughly dissolved. Gently stir into chocolate mixture together with whipped cream. Lastly fold in stiffly beaten egg whites.

Pour into individual moulds, chill for at least 1 hour or overnight until set.

Rub raspberries through a fine nylon sieve or puree in a food processor. Stir in icing sugar a little at a time until a fairly thick puree is made, with sweetness to taste.

to serve: Either turn mousselines out on to a serving plate and carefully pour a little of the coulis around the sides of the plate, or serve them in their dishes with a little of the raspberry coulis poured over. Serve decorated with fresh raspberries and mint leaves.

serves 2 - 3 large portions or 4 small ones
preparation time 10 - 15 minutes

ingredients

- 75g white chocolate
- 4 tblspns milk
- 1 tblspn Irish cream liqueur
- 2 teaspns gelatine
  or 3 leaves gelatine, prepared according to pack instructions
- 2 egg whites, stiffly beaten
- 150ml carton double or whipping cream, whipped until stiff
- 75 - 125g raspberries, washed and hulled
- approximately 2 tblspns icing sugar

what about...
quick tips - that make life easier:

Refresh potato crisps, corn chips and biscuits by heating in the microwave on HIGH power for 15 seconds before serving.

For quick nibbles - cover the top of a plate of corn chips or potato snacks with grated cheese and a sprinkle of paprika pepper. Heat on HIGH for 1 - 2 minutes until cheese melts - delicious!

Soften butter and soft cheeses for spreading by heating on HIGH for 15 seconds.

Put oranges and lemons in the microwave oven and heat on HIGH for 15 seconds - this makes the fruit easier to squeeze and also helps yield more juice.

Fruit like avocado pears, ordinary pears and mangoes can be ripened quickly. Set in the middle of the microwave oven and heat on MEDIUM for 30 seconds. Leave to cool, but use the same day otherwise they will over-ripen.

If you have left over coffee made with ground coffee beans, keep it in the refrigerator - heat 1 cupful at a time in the microwave for 1 $\frac{1}{2}$ minutes. Results - fresh tasting coffee - instantly!

Add fresh life to dried fruit by placing in a small oven-proof bowl, sprinkle with water, fruit juice or sherry, cover bowl and heat for 30 seconds.

If you have problems igniting the brandy on a Christmas pudding - pour a measure into a glass, heat in the microwave for 15 seconds before pouring over pudding. It should ignite instantly once flamed.

To blanch and skin nuts: Pour 300ml of boiling water over nuts, set in an oven proof bowl. Heat on HIGH power for 1 minute. Drain well; skins will slip off easily.

When freezing left over soup, line a soup bowl with a plastic cook-bag. Pour in soup - enough for one portion. Once frozen, the bag can be removed from the bowl, sealed and labeled for storage. While the bowl can be put back into use.
To heat soup, remove plastic bag and place frozen soup into bowl, it can be thawed, and reheated in this bowl - and is just the right amount for one serving!

Toasted desiccated coconut, chopped or sliced nuts and seeds (e.g. sesame) not only add extra colour but are great for all sorts of toppings. Spread coconut, nuts or seeds on to a glass oven-proof plate. Heat on HIGH for 2 - 3 minutes until they start to brown. Stir frequently during cooking so that they do not burn. Leave to cool before using.

Tomatoes and peppers can be peeled easily if they are set on a glass oven-proof plate then heated in the microwave on HIGH power for 1 minute.

Warm golden syrup, treacle, honey or the hard to get at ends of jams and ketchups in the jar for 30 seconds. You'll find they are much easier to get out of the jar then, and make weighing out a breeze.

For a quick jelly, place a 135g jelly block in a glass measuring jug, add just 150ml of hot water, set in the microwave oven and heat on HIGH for 1 minute, stir well to disperse jelly, top up with 400ml very cold water or fruit juice. Refrigerate until set.

Poppadums and commercial prawn crackers cook perfectly in the microwave oven. Spread evenly over the glass turntable or oven rack and heat for 30 - 60 seconds at a time, until well risen and cooked through.

Warm up to 4 dinner plates at a time before any meal, by setting on turntable or cooking rack under cooking pots. Heat given off during the cooking, will heat the plates - purely by conduction.

Melt chocolate by placing broken pieces into an oven-proof bowl. Heat on MEDIUM for up to 5 minutes, stirring well after every 1 minute. Stop cooking when chocolate appears glossy. Stir well before using, but do not over-heat as the chocolate will go grainy and burn, if this should happen, beat in 1 teaspn of solid vegetable fat (not butter) and use immediately.

Make great lemonade by heating together 1 cup water, 1 large piece of lemon peel and 1 - 2 teaspns sugar on HIGH for 2 minutes. Stir in the juice of 1 lemon. Serve hot in winter or chilled in summer.

Refresh bread rolls by setting them on a piece of absorbent kitchen paper and heating for 10 - 15 seconds (for 2 large rolls).
Place 5 - 6 rolls in serving basket, heat for 1 minute. Don't heat for any longer, otherwise they start to steam and go stale immediately.

Decant cheap red wine into a glass jug. Heat for 30 seconds to both take the chill off it and make a smoother flavour.

Dry fresh garden herbs in the mircowave - place washed leaves between 2 pieces of kitchen paper. Cook on HIGH for 2 - 3 minutes - turning frequently until herbs have dried out. Store in a sealed jar for use later.

some questions... answered...

question: Why do bread rolls, croissants and bread loaves go hard on cooling after warming through or defrosting in the microwave oven?

answer: They have been over-heated. Flour products contain a lot of moisture which evaporates during microwave heating, so although they taste and smell pleasant when immediately taken out of the oven, on cooling the bread goes hard. In other words, it has gone 'stale'.

remedy: Use a lower power setting, for a minimal amount of time. Use stale bread to make breadcrumbs and store in the freezer for future use.

question: Why are my cakes uncooked in the centre?

answer: It could be one of the following reasons:
- The cooking container was not large enough or the incorrect shape for the quantity of cake mixture, so all the cake mixture did not get thoroughly cooked.
- Insufficient cooking time.
- The cooking container was not elevated, with the result that microwaves could not penetrate evenly throughout the cake mix.

remedy: Return cake to the oven and continue to cook on MEDIUM for 1 minute at a time.

question: Why does the pastry in pies and quiches go soggy on reheating?

answer: If the pie has been overheated, steam from the hot filling will be absorbed by the pastry and make it soggy.

remedy: Always stand pastries on absorbent kitchen paper to absorb excess moisture. Be careful not to overheat, as this can also burn the filling and some times toughen the pastry.

question: My sauces are often lumpy or they boil over during cooking. What am I doing wrong?

answer: All types of sauces cook quickly and simply in the microwave oven. But make sure you: Use a large high sided oven-proof jug for cooking to prevent the liquid from boiling over. Stir the sauce at 1 minute intervals so that the flour disperses quickly in the liquid before it gets too hot. Beat well once the liquid has reached boiling point, to add gloss to the sauce.

question: When cooking chicken breasts or thighs in a sauce why does the sauce go thin and watery?

answer: Chicken meat contains a lot of moisture. During conventional cooking most of this is drawn off as steam, so it goes unnoticed. In the microwave oven, the heat is inside the food and doesn't evaporate, so it seeps into the sauce, thinning it down.

remedy: Place chicken in a well-covered dish and cook on MEDIUM to MEDIUM HIGH. A more gentle cook will prevent excessive moisture loss. Stir the sauce well before serving.

question: Can I really use aluminium foil and metal dishes in my microwave oven?

answer: Yes, but with caution. Microwaves cannot penetrate through metal, so bounce off them. If you wrap food in foil and put it in the microwave oven, it will not cook, as no microwaves can penetrate through the foil. The food will therefore remain cold and uncooked.
However, shallow foil dishes are great to cook meals that cannot be stirred, such as lasagne. As the microwaves can only penetrate through the top of the food, (they just bounce off the sides and base of the dish). The food cooks much more evenly - the middle cooks as quickly as the corners, so you do not get heated and burned corners

while the centre is still frozen. Metal edged plates and cups etc should not be used in the microwave oven as the metal will soon disintegrate with frequent use, however shallow metal dishes, set on china or glass plates are acceptable, as the metal is separated from the metal rack or metal shelves by something other than metal. Aluminium foil can be used to shield the delicate and thin ends of food to assist with even cooking, such as the heads and tails of whole fish, the thin ends of a leg of lamb or chicken drumsticks.

question: Why don't microwaves pass through the oven door?

answer: There is a very fine metal mesh in the oven door which deflects the waves back into the oven.

question: Is it more efficient and economical to heat a cup of water in the microwave oven or a kettle?

answer: A kettle, so if boiling water or stock is required for a recipe, use a kettle to heat the water.

question: My manual refers to variable power - what is this?

answer: Variable power is the name given to the function of the various heat settings. For example HIGH, MEDIUM HIGH, MEDIUM or MEDIUM LOW.
If HIGH power is selected, the oven operates 100% of the time. If MEDIUM is selected the oven is only 'on' for 50% of the time, but the food inside it is still cooking. Variable power makes the cooking extremely efficient and environmentally friendly as the power usage is dramatically reduced.

index

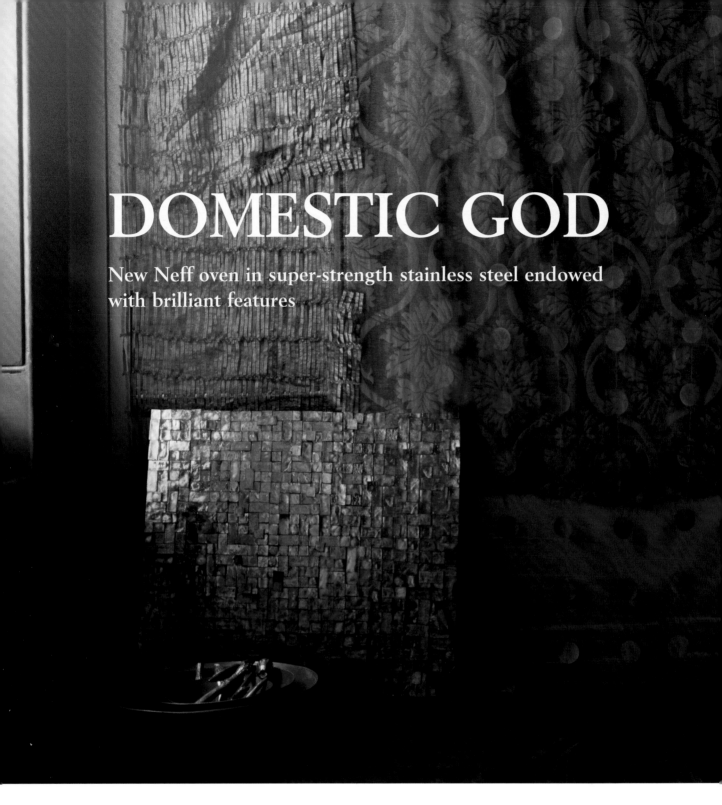

DOMESTIC GOD

New Neff oven in super-strength stainless steel endowed with brilliant features

DOMESTIC GODDESS

- **Multi-tasks magnificently.** The CircoTherm® system lets you cook sweet and savoury at the same time without mingling flavours.

- **Doesn't have to bother opening the oven to see cooking-in-progress.** Innovative halogen lights inside the oven door fill every corner with bright, white light.

- **Miracle worker – cooks to perfection.** Stirring and basting made simple. (New state of the art shelves extend way out of the oven for easiest-ever access.)

- **Wouldn't waste precious time cleaning the oven** – CeramiClean™ liners clean themselves as they go along.

For a free brochure call 0870 513 3090 www.neff.co.uk